The Mexican Congress
Old Player, New Power

Significant Issues Series

Timely books presenting current CSIS research and analysis of interest to the academic, business, government, and policy communities.

Managing editor: Roberta L. Howard

The **Center for Strategic and International Studies (CSIS)**, established in 1962, is a private, tax-exempt institution focusing on international public policy issues. Its research is nonpartisan and nonproprietary.

CSIS is dedicated to policy analysis and impact. It seeks to inform and shape selected policy decisions in government and the private sector to meet the increasingly complex and difficult global challenges that leaders will confront in this new century. It achieves this mission in four ways: by generating strategic analysis that is anticipatory and interdisciplinary; by convening policymakers and other influential parties to assess key issues; by building structures for policy action; and by developing leaders.

CSIS does not take specific public policy positions. Accordingly, all views, positions, and conclusions expressed in this publication should be understood to be solely those of the authors.

The CSIS Press

Center for Strategic and International Studies
1800 K Street, N.W., Washington, D.C. 20006
Telephone: (202) 887-0200   Fax: (202) 775-3199
E-mail: books@csis.org   Web site: http://www.csis.org/

The Mexican Congress
Old Player, New Power

L U I S　　C A R L O S　　U G A L D E

Foreword by Armand B. Peschard-Sverdrup

THE CSIS PRESS

**Center for Strategic
and International Studies**

Washington, D.C.

Significant Issues Series, Volume XXII, Number 4
Printed on recycled paper in the United States of America
Cover design by Robert L. Wiser, Archetype Press, Washington, D.C.

04   03   02   01   00   5   4   3   2   1

ISSN 0736-7136
ISBN 0-89206-382-3

Library of Congress Cataloging-in-Publication Data
Ugalde, Luis Carlos, 1966–
   The Mexican congress : old player, new power / by Luis Carlos Ugalde ;
foreword by Armand B. Peschard-Sverdrup.
      p. cm.—(Significant issues series ; v. 22, no. 4)
   Includes bibliographical references and index.
   ISBN 0-89206-382-3
   1. Mexico. Congreso. Camara de Diputados—Powers and duties. 2. Separation of
powers—Mexico. 3. Legislative oversight—Mexico. 4. Governmental investigations—Mexico. I. Title. II. Series.

JL1265 .U38 2000
328.72'072—dc21   00-011772

CONTENTS

LIST OF FIGURES AND TABLES

FOREWORD

Armand B. Peschard-Sverdrup

As Mexico leaves behind its political experience of the twentieth century and sets forth to chart a new course for this century, it does so having emerged as a nation that—by the will of its own people—has achieved electoral democracy through a peaceful and orderly process. The result is a remarkable testament to a nation that has lived under the shadow of one-party rule longer than any other nation in contemporary history.

Mexico's democratic awakening did not occur overnight, however. It is the result of a protracted journey that commenced many, many years ago. The historic and much publicized outcomes of the 1997 and 2000 elections—after which the Institutional Revolutionary Party (PRI) watched its control over Congress and subsequently the presidency slip away—are but milestones in a journey that is still ongoing.

With a single party having controlled Congress and the presidency for the last seven decades, one of the legacies left behind has been a form of government that has concentrated excessive power in the office of the president. Hence the term *presidencialismo*. Even though this form of government has been in part an outgrowth of one-party rule, it too was rooted in the grim memories of Mexico's turbulent revolutionary history. Historians note that Mexico's strong national government was a natural evolution, as the country sought

Armand B. Peschard-Sverdrup is the director of the Mexico Project at CSIS.

to escape the perils of regionalism that repeatedly threatened its political stability.

While *presidencialismo* may have ensured Mexico's longstanding political stability, regrettably it also undermined the virtues that come with separation of powers—among them, oversight and accountability—particularly between the executive and legislative branches of government. As a result, until only three years ago, the role of the Mexican Congress was principally symbolic in nature—it was what is commonly referred to as "a rubber stamp Congress." Only since 1997, when the two main opposition parties—the National Action Party and the Democratic Revolutionary Party—combined to form a majority in the lower house (Chamber of Deputies), did the Mexican Congress slowly begin to evolve and conduct business as a true legislature.

The journey upon which Mexico is embarking is bound to be a complex and an arduous one. It must now include the task of transforming its form of government to reflect the country's new political reality—from one that concentrated excessive power in the office of the president to one that is more pluralistic and representative of the needs of Mexican society as a whole.

It is against this historical backdrop that the CSIS Mexico Project is proud to publish this very thorough, insightful, timely, and balanced analysis of the Mexican Congress by Luis Carlos Ugalde. Because of his numerous years spent studying the Mexican Congress, Ugalde brings a wealth of knowledge as well as experience to the subject. He also comes to his subject from the unique vantage point of someone who simultaneously interacted with the legislature through the various positions he held within the executive branch; yet he has maintained his scholarly objectivity in his account. What's more, Ugalde exemplifies the generation that is likely to figure predominantly in charting Mexico's new course.

Ugalde's study is the result of exhaustive field research covering the period between 1970 and 2000. This is a monumental undertaking, considering that—as the author himself points out—the Mexican Congress as a bureaucracy did not even maintain congressional voting records from years past. Nonetheless, Ugalde persevered in his search and has succeeded in quantifiably illustrating and explaining how—and why—the role and power of the Mexican Congress has evolved in some cases, but not in others.

The underlying impediment to a more effective Congress in Mexico, according to Ugalde, is the fact that consecutive reelection has been prohibited since 1933. He contends that, as a result, Congress has become a revolving door that perpetuates, and in some ways promotes, the inexperience of its members. Individuals are, for the most part, elected to Congress with little or no legislative experience and are forced out at the conclusion of their terms, just as they have acquired such experience. Specialists in the field have pointed out that this limitation is exacerbated by the fact that congressional terms for deputies and senators—three and six years, respectively—are not even staggered, resulting in a complete turnover in both chambers at the end of legislators' terms in office. Ugalde believes that this situation has atrophied the oversight capabilities and functioning of the Mexican Congress—and even Congress members' will to exert their legitimate power—and he presents compelling evidence to substantiate this conclusion. Moreover, the constitutional ban on reelection has resulted in a relatively weak legislature, which, when contrasted with Mexico's *presidencialismo*, is clearly an inadequate counterweight.

Furthermore, in a political system with no possibility of reelection—coupled with the omnipotent-like power of the presidency—legislators were increasingly compelled to rely on the president and his partisan powers in order to advance their political careers. This situation resulted in two adverse effects. First, it created congressional accountability to the president—as opposed to the state-level constituencies Congress members "supposedly" represented. This is what Ugalde refers to as "reversed accountability." Second, the system basically undermined the relevance of Congress, demeaning the stature of its members both in their own eyes and in the eyes of the public at large, their constituents included.

Ugalde also delves into the intricate details of Mexico's budgetary process—from the Treasury Ministry's initial submission of the budget to Congress through to the actual floor vote and beyond, that is, its attempts to verify the data included and monitor expenditures. He examines how the PRI's chairmanship of the Chamber's Budget Committee until 1997 influenced the budget process over the years, and how the process has evolved since the opposition assumed leadership of the committee. It is a fascinating period, particularly because only three short years ago, in 1997, the Budget Committee became the first battleground of the country's new political era. It is the arena in which Mexican Congress members from all political parties—with admittedly limited expertise in the business of government—experienced, for the very first time, the trial-by-fire birth of negotiation, bargaining, and consensus building, while at the same time facing the daunting task of reviewing, amending, and passing the budget just a month into the start of their first (for most) legislative session. This is a task that becomes ever so pressing in light of the fact that Mexican legislators do not have the luxury of resorting to a "continuing resolution" in the event that consensus is not reached—as is the case in the United States.

The author also describes how the increasing presence of opposition party members in Congress has led to reinventing the legislative structure in order to either institute or strengthen the congressional oversight function. To illustrate this point he looks at the proposed replacement of the *Contaduría Mayor de Hacienda* (CMH) with the much more powerful *Auditoría Superior de la Federación* (ASF), which is expected to be officially created by the newly installed 58th Legislature. The role of these offices within the Chamber of Deputies—comparable to the General Accounting Office in the United States Congress—is to oversee the use and effectiveness of public finances and enterprises in Mexico, and the author explores the Treasury Accounting Office's past efforts—both its successes and failures—in some detail.

Ugalde also highlights the fact that—in spite of a 1977 constitutional reform authorizing their formation—since 1978, only seven investigative committees have been created to monitor government expenditures and to examine the operations of public enterprises. He outlines the history of their creation and reports on the results of their efforts—both positive and negative—and suggests reasons for any perceived inadequacy or ineffectiveness. The low number of such committees and the lackluster results of their investigations clearly indicate that legislative oversight has been insufficient and has partially contributed to a flagrant sense of impunity among certain government officials.

In sum, the book is unquestionably a comprehensive diagnosis of what went wrong with the Mexican Congress. In addition, it describes the fine-tuning that has taken place since the opposition assumed a greater role. Hence, old player, new power. The book is a "must read" for those who want to appreciate the magnitude of its challenge as the Mexican Congress attempts to strengthen itself from an institutional standpoint. This is an indispensable task that must be carried out by Congress itself, while it also tends to its role in the governance of Mexico. This is a feat that, on its own, is complex, and it is further compounded by the fact that both branches of government, the presidency as well as the Congress, need to adjust to the shift in power—one relinquishing and the other acquiring. As if that were not enough, Mexico must also navigate the extremely sensitive alternation in the power of the Mexican presidency following the heralded victory of Vicente Fox Quesada. All these are vital journeys that will determine the future of the Mexican people.

The CSIS Mexico Project is extremely grateful to the Smith Richardson Foundation for its financial support for this particular study, and to the William and Flora Hewlett Foundation for overall financial support of the work carried out by the Mexico Project.

PREFACE

Luis Carlos Ugalde

MEXICO'S DEMOCRACY HAS EVOLVED RAPIDLY IN A MATTER OF YEARS. After decades during which one party controlled most elected offices in Mexico, as of December 2000 an opposition party will head the executive branch. Mexican democracy was not born as a result of Vicente Fox's victory in the July 2000 presidential election, however. Rather, it was a consequence of gradual and overdue political reforms and negotiations among parties and political actors dating back to the late 1970s. Since the mid-1990s, opposition parties had been increasingly victorious in taking over elected offices, including governorships, state assemblies, and, in 1997, the majority share in the Chamber of Deputies. The triumph of the National Action Party's candidate for the presidency in July 2000 is only the last step in the process of democratization, and it reflects the consolidation of Mexico's electoral system—albeit with imperfections and weaknesses that still need to be fine-tuned.

With the shift in political power, a pertinent concern is the degree to which the new pluralism—in both the executive and legislative branches—will actually bring about democratic governability as well as increased accountability on the part of elected government officials. If the Institutional Revolutionary Party (PRI) was blamed for the concentration of power in the presidency, the party's defeat at the polls in July 2000 has naturally created expectations that the new government not only will be accountable to the Congress and the people of Mexico but also will be more effective in meeting society's needs. Increased pluralism does not automatically translate into a system of checks and balances, however, much less into effective government.

Understanding the causes that led Congress to abdicate its oversight responsibilities during the years that the PRI controlled both branches of government can, by contrast, shed light on the likely impact of recent events on the future of legislative oversight in Mexico. The larger presence of the opposition in Congress—coupled with the turnover in the party affiliation of the presidency—is bound to have a significant effect on Congress members' motivations and efforts. Analyzing the reasons for Congress's ineffectiveness in the past can also suggest what reforms need to be enacted to strengthen Congress once it has achieved plurality. If studying the Mexican Congress was considered a somewhat irrelevant undertaking just a generation ago, today it has become an indispensable tool for understanding and anticipating the country's political development.

In this book, I have tried to analyze the specific case of the Chamber of Deputies in Mexico, because, over the past few decades, the Chamber has not been an effective counterbalance to the executive branch. Indeed, between 1970 and 1997, the lower house of Congress acted more as an agent of the presidency than as a supervisor of its actions. The imbalance contributed to the executive branch's low level of political accountability and allowed, by omission, the spread of corruption and mismanagement. Even though Mexico's Constitution and secondary laws grant the Chamber sufficient powers to oversee the government, in practice there has been a gap between what the written law establishes and what has actually been monitored.

One of the main areas defining the relationship between the executive and legislative branches of government in Mexico—as in most countries of the world—is the oversight of public finances. For most of the period between 1970 and 1997, the Chamber of Deputies was ineffective in supervising public expenditures and at times even blocked the attempts of opposition parties to monitor particular agencies—agencies that were later found to be riddled with administrative mismanagement and corruption. It would be wrong to argue that insufficient and weak legislative oversight was the principal cause of government corruption, but it is reasonable to suggest that inadequate supervision contributed to the lack of accountability that characterized the executive branch over most of the period of this study. In turn, this lack of accountability facilitated the government's misbehavior and malfeasance.

The most relevant variable that helps to explain the ineffectiveness of legislative control can be found in the motivations that shaped deputies' behavior. Prohibited from running for consecutive reelection, Mexican legislators had to seek promotion to other offices after their terms had expired. In Mexico, because the chief executive had ample power to select his party's (PRI) candidates to most elected offices, deputies were compelled to please and lobby the president, who was the principal source of support for advancing their political careers (at least until very recently). Consequently, the direction of accountability was reversed—from legislators' constituencies, which mattered little because they were unable to reelect their representatives, to the chief executive, who could easily promote the political careers of loyal followers.

Because of the PRI's long-term hold on the majority of Chamber seats, this pattern of what is called "reversed accountability" discouraged PRI members' incentives to oversee the executive branch. The opposition grew in strength, however, to the point of becoming the Chamber's majority in 1997. Since then, the frequency of legislative supervision has increased, as has the Chamber's criticism of government mismanagement. Although the effectiveness of these legislative initiatives is still very limited, the fact that the Chamber has begun to exercise its legal authority to monitor the administration's activities and review its financial operations has contributed to increased accountability on the part of the government. This study attempts to shed light on the political causes that might explain the recent change in legislative oversight efforts.

To illustrate concrete cases of the relations between the executive and legislative branches in Mexico, I have chosen to examine in detail two specific areas of congressional activity: (1) legislative oversight of public expenditures, particularly the way the Mexican *Contaduría Mayor de Hacienda* (the auditing office of the Chamber of Deputies) reviews the public spending process in Mexico; and (2) the performance of the Chamber's investigative committees, which are created on an ad hoc basis to review the operations of public enterprises. This study analyzes the work done in both areas between 1970 and 2000.

The book is divided into seven chapters. Chapter 1 contains a brief review of existing academic approaches to the analysis of congressional behavior in general, both in Mexico and in the United States, and also suggests a framework for analyzing the Mexican case. Chapters 2 and 3 present case studies that describe and examine how actual legislative oversight was conducted in Mexico from 1970 to 2000. In addition, chapter 2 offers a detailed account of the budgetary process, as well as the specific oversight activities conducted by the *Contaduría Mayor de Hacienda;* and chapter 3 details the creation, performance, and results of investigative committees since passage of a constitutional amendment providing for these committees in 1977. The ineffectiveness and infrequency of the Chamber's oversight activities are evident from the accounts described in both chapters. Chapters 4 and 5 explore the possible causes for the lack of an effective system of legislative oversight in Mexico. In particular, Chapter 4 examines the institution of nonconsecutive reelection and its effect on the experience and professionalism of Mexican deputies. Chapter 5 proposes the hypothesis of reversed accountability as a new way to explain how nonreelectability—in conjunction with the partisan powers of the Mexican presidency—has reversed the direction of political accountability of Mexican lawmakers. Chapter 6 explains how the strengthening of the opposition within the Chamber of Deputies, especially since 1997, has contributed to an increased level of legislative oversight. Finally, chapter 7 summarizes the discussion, offers some solutions to the problems that have been described, and proposes recommendations for the future.

ACKNOWLEDGMENTS

THIS BOOK IS THE RESULT OF MANY YEARS OF RESEARCH. FOR GUIDING me through this endeavor, I am especially grateful to my professors at Columbia University who became my mentors and were also readers and advisers for this work: Giovanni Sartori and Douglas Chalmers. I also would like to thank Robert Kaufman, who helped proofread the original work and provided feedback and suggestions. I am grateful to M. Delal Baer, chair of the Mexico Project at the Center for Strategic and International Studies (CSIS) in Washington, D.C., for her interest and support in publishing this work. In particular, I want to express my thanks to Armand Peschard-Sverdrup, director of the Mexico Project at CSIS, for his kind and enthusiastic support; for the time he spent reviewing the manuscript, making valuable suggestions, and writing the foreword; and, above all, for his patience and commitment in bringing this editorial project to a conclusion. Kristopher Bengston, the research assistant for the CSIS Mexico Project, was also very helpful during the editorial process.

Since I have also made an inroad into the Mexican government over the last few years, I want to express my gratitude to Jesús Reyes Heroles, who has always stimulated me and allowed me to conduct academic research and other activities not directly related to my responsibilities at work, and from whom I have learned the virtue of being both intellectually and personally honest. I am grateful as well to John Vázquez, Roger Wallace, Allert Brown-Gort, Paula Bocaz,

David Morrill, and Bita Lanys for reading the entire manuscript and providing suggestions for improving my English. In particular, I want to acknowledge and stress Bita's detailed copyediting, talent, professionalism, and kindness; she made an important contribution by improving not only the grammar and syntax of the manuscript but also its substance in many important ways. Her timely response to editorial needs made this endeavor smooth and pleasant. In addition, Marina Spindler was kind in helping to translate the bibliography into English and formatting the many tables included. I am most grateful as well to Ena Victoria Rosas for her ceaseless care, professionalism, and support in updating data, correcting tables, and suggesting changes to the content and substance of the work. I will always appreciate her friendly and unwavering commitment to this project.

Finally, I want to thank my family and friends for their support in various ways over the past few years. Along the last steps on this road, Lia has been an inspiring part of my life, and I thank her for her patience and her encouragement. I hope all these efforts will contribute in some small way to improving the political debate about Mexico and will help to influence the political reforms that are needed in my country.

CHAPTER ONE

THEORETICAL FRAMEWORK

MEXICAN POLITICS IS IN FLUX AND HAS BEEN SO FOR THE PAST FEW years. After many years of electoral reforms and trial-and-error attempts on the part of government, political parties, the media, and other major players, electoral democracy has become a reality. But Mexican democracy was not born in July 2000, when an opposition candidate won the presidency for the first time in Mexico's modern history. The electoral outcome arising on that date was simply a reflection of a long and sometimes overdue process that was establishing a credible and transparent system of political competition in Mexico.

Before the arrival of expanded democratic representation, the presidency had been the focus of political bargaining and representation in Mexico. Other political actors—Congress, for example—had a limited voice and little influence in the policymaking process. With the emergence of plurality, most notably since 1997, Congress has become a principal player in the Mexican political arena. In that year, for the first time in its modern history, Mexico began experiencing a divided government, in which the president's party—the Institutional Revolutionary Party (PRI)—did not enjoy an absolute majority in the Chamber of Deputies. That fact began to change the logic and nature of relations between the executive branch and the legislative branch and led to unprecedented forms of political bargaining and compromise.

The outcome of the July 2000 presidential election will produce the second consecutive period during which the country will experience a divided government, but this time with a non-PRI president at the helm: Vicente Fox will be the chief executive, but his party—the National Action Party (PAN)—will not enjoy a plurality of seats in either house of Congress. This situation will once again stimulate unimaginable dynamics in relations between both branches of government. Will a PAN president behave differently than his PRI predecessors did when dealing with his party's congressional delegations? Will the deputies and senators from the PAN act in a way that is independent of the president's mandate or will they act in a way that will please the chief executive? What will be the attitude of opposition members in Congress, especially those of the PRI, toward the executive branch?

The Mexican Congress has become a key player in the Mexican political system, and its role in the years to come will undoubtedly shape the nature of Mexico's presidential system. Even though the study of the Mexican Congress might have been considered a relatively unimportant undertaking in the past, it now appears that the analysis can be applied and used effectively not only to understand the country's political development but also to anticipate the path it will follow.

LITERATURE ON THE MEXICAN CONGRESS

Until recently, the Mexican Congress had received little scholarly attention because of its secondary role in the nation's politics. Except for legal and historical analyses, bibliography on this topic was almost nonexistent. No appropriate analytical frameworks had been proposed to facilitate the study of legislative behavior in Mexico, and databases documenting congressional activities were lacking. According to Lujambio, "the postrevolutionary political situation, with absolute majorities and pluralities for only one party, which was that of the president and governors, … produced weak legislative bodies and a systematic neglect by Mexican political scientists of the study of the legislative branch." Nevertheless, the same author pointed out that the increasing pluralism of Mexican legislatures "has been generating an ever-deepening interest in legislative dynamics among political scientists."[1]

Even though recent years have witnessed a resurgence of interest in studying the Mexican Congress, the research remains scarce and mostly limited to works that are basically descriptive. In 1972, Rudolph de la Garza, perhaps the first scholar to have conducted a comprehensive analytical study of the Mexican Chamber of Deputies, complained that "no scholar has subjected the Mexican legislature to rigorous analysis."[2] He wrote that "studies by American scholars on the Mexican Congress have been limited to one detailed description of the formal powers of each Chamber and one cursory analysis of congressional campaigning…. Most students of Mexican politics, on learning that the Mexican Congress does not operate in the way they believe the United States Congress operates, have concluded that the Mexican legislature is unworthy of further study and largely irrelevant to Mexican politics."[3]

Nevertheless, attention seems to be growing now that the legislative branch of government—after decades of passive behavior—has gained momentum as a principal political force. The July 2000 presidential election has only increased the importance of Congress: voters elected a member of the National Action Party to the presidency but a plurality of non-PAN candidates to Congress. Consequently, academic interest has increased proportionately. Yet the scholarly research remains scarce, less analytical, and more general than studies of the U.S. Congress. Current academic research on this topic in Mexico consists of historical studies, legal studies, and studies of Congress's economic and budgetary powers as well as the behavioral consequences of the 1917 Constitution's nonconsecutive reelection clause.

Historical Studies

Historical studies analyze the origins and evolution of today's Mexican Congress: the 1812 Spanish Constitution of Cádiz, the 1824 and 1857 Mexican Constitutions, and the most immediate antecedent—

the 1917 Constitution.[4] Most of this research explores the development of the Mexican Congress, with emphasis on its "parliamentary" experience during the nineteenth century.[5] For example, Reynaldo Sordo's book analyzed the political struggle that took place between *centralistas* and *federalistas* during the 1833–41 period.[6] Some historians have studied the impact of the 1857 Constitution on relations between the executive and legislative branches during the *República restaurada*; Emilio Rabasa's book, *La Constitución y la dictadura*, published in 1912, is worth mentioning in this regard. In this work, Rabasa criticized the institutional and legal framework laid out by the 1857 Constitution, because it granted Congress ample powers over the executive branch, which resulted in a permanent conflict between both branches of government as well as inapplicability of the law. In Rabasa's opinion, the Constitution of 1857 established a form of political organization for Mexico's presidential system that was both contradictory and counterproductive.[7] Other relevant works of this period include Daniel Cosío Villegas's *La Constitución de 1857 y sus críticos* (published in 1957),[8] and Frank A. Knapp's *Parliamentary Government and the Mexican Constitution of 1857: A Forgotten Phase of Mexican Political History* (published in 1953).[9]

Legal Studies

Produced by lawyers and public administrators, these studies emphasize the constitutional and legal foundations of congressional activity, as well as any powers granted to Congress to control and oversee the executive branch. Usually, these works are descriptive and focus exclusively on legal considerations.[10] Worth mentioning is Felipe Tena's *Derecho constitucional mexicano*, which gives an account of the legal framework surrounding executive-legislative relations, a description of the organization and functioning of Congress, and a detailed analysis of Congress's powers to legislate and oversee the executive branch.[11] Another classic book is Jorge Carpizo's *El Presidencialismo mexicano*, published in 1978, in which the author coined the term "metaconstitutional powers" to describe the partisan powers PRI presidents had to select candidates to run for congressional seats, for governorships, and for the presidency. According to Carpizo, metaconstitutional powers are not contained in any formalized or written norm, but they nevertheless provided a powerful means for the president to predominate as the single most important and powerful actor in Mexican politics.[12]

Studies of Economic and Budgetary Powers

Some scholars have studied the legislative functions of Congress in economic and financial matters, as well as the role of the Chamber of Deputies in the budgetary process (as does this study).[13] Although the executive branch has been a driving force in the planning and implementation of economic development in Mexico over this century, the Constitution grants ample authority to Congress to oversee and legislate matters related to economic planning and financial regulation. Similarly, although the budget has always been drafted by the administration, the Constitution also grants Congress sufficient power to supervise and approve budgets submitted by the executive branch.

Studies of the Behavioral Consequences of Nonconsecutive Reelection

In recent years, a small group of researchers has begun to analyze the behavioral implications of the nonconsecutive reelection clause applied to Mexican lawmakers. (This book is concerned with this topic as well; it is explored in detail in chapter 4.) All these scholars agree that the inability to be reelected has reduced Mexican deputies' sense of accountability to their constituencies, because legislators do not feel the need to respond to voters in order to advance their political careers. Some studies also stress the effects of nonreelectability on the lack of experience and professionalism of members of the Mexican Chamber of Deputies.[14]

Over the past few years, academic arguments stressing the perverse effects of nonreelectability on the accountability and professionalism of members of the Mexican Congress have permeated the political debate, leading many politicians to embrace the idea of reinstating the reelection of deputies as a means of strengthening the Mexican Congress. Indeed, one primary proposal expounded by Vicente Fox and his team just after the July 2000 election was the intention to introduce legislation—as soon as possible after taking office—that would permit consecutive reelection of Congress members and of mayors.

LITERATURE ON THE U.S. CONGRESS

In contrast to the scarcity of research on the Mexican Congress, academic literature on the U.S. Congress is prolific, with hundreds of scholarly articles, books, and dissertations produced every year. A specialized journal, *Legislative Studies Quarterly,* serves as a forum for experts to discuss issues related to Congress. Many nonacademic publications, some produced by the U.S. Congress itself, disseminate information about the legislative agenda and congressional activities. In addition, every professional association of political scientists in the United States has sections specializing in congressional studies.

It was after World War II that scholars saw the emergence of the first generation of studies—mostly descriptive and static—dealing with the "textbook Congress," as it was labeled by many. These studies characterized the U.S. Congress as having "a strong committee system, powerful committee chairs, a rigid adherence to the seniority system ... and party leadership based, for the most part, on personality and persuasion rather than on sanctions and coercion."[15] According to Shepsle, the equilibrium that existed within the U.S. Congress in the 1950s—when committees were the center of political activity, seniority was unquestionable, and committee jurisdictions and limits were stable and easily identifiable—began to break down in the 1960s and 1970s as a result of various processes of political change. These included (1) the experience of unified government in the 1960s (Kennedy, Johnson, and the Democrats); (2) political activism by many first-year legislators, who began to revive the old ranks of Congress during that decade; (3) the increasing questioning of the seniority system and of the authority of committee chairs; and

(4) the decentralization and shift of authority and resources from committees to subcommittees.[16] Therefore, by the late 1960s, the heuristic ability of the "textbook Congress" approach had decreased substantially.

In the early 1970s, the U.S. Congress received renewed attention, as scholars attempted to explain legislative behavior inside Congress as the outcome of external factors—in particular, the way constituents' preferences, needs, and demands were able to shape legislators' behavior. More than any other study, David Mayhew's book, entitled *Congress: The Electoral Connection* (published in 1974), was responsible for bringing the curtain down on the concept of the "textbook Congress," inspiring scholars to conduct new research along the instrumental rationality lines Mayhew had explored.[17] In this new approach, the unit of analysis became the individual legislators as they aspired to be reelected to office. Mayhew argued that what legislators "did both inside and outside the Congress could be explained by their re-election concerns. Specifically, members engaged in credit-claiming, advertising, and position-taking activities as a way to ensure their re-election."[18]

This approach to legislative studies generated a subfield that deals with congressional oversight of the bureaucracy. In general, the academic literature on this topic explores the factors that increase the possibility of congressional oversight being conducted as a result of the response of "rational legislators" to institutional incentives. The research along these lines uses surveys and interviews to infer legislators' preferences as well as to explain how external factors shape legislators' motivations to oversee the administration's activities.[19] As an example, Morris Ogul's 1976 book, *Congress Oversees the Bureaucracy*, was one of the first comprehensive and systematic studies specifically dedicated to congressional oversight.[20] Ogul analyzed the factors that increase or decrease the chances of legislative oversight, which he defined as "behavior by legislators and their staffs, individually or collectively, which results in an impact, intended or not, on bureaucratic behavior."[21] For Ogul, oversight is most likely to occur when there is a series of conditioning factors, which he called "opportunity factors," because they tend either to promote the potential for oversight or to limit its possibility. Some of these factors include the following:

1. Legal authority: Legal powers support oversight activity; the absence of such authority can handicap effective oversight.

2. Staff resources: Access to staff facilitates oversight; but the amount of oversight conducted does not depend primarily on the size of available staff. "Adequate staff is a necessary precondition to oversight but is not a sufficient one."[23]

3. Party affiliation: Members of the opposition party are more likely to engage in oversight activity than are members of the president's party.

4. Visibility of "the issue at hand": The greater the visibility of an issue that can be subject to congressional oversight and review, the more likely it is to be overseen, given the political rewards that publicity offers to lawmakers.

For Ogul, oversight depends on "how rewarded it is as compared to other activities legislators can engage in."[23] Sometimes, oversight helps to achieve political visibility or credit for criticizing government corruption or mismanagement and thus becomes a vehicle for gaining public trust and approval. At other times, the opportunity costs of oversight can be too high, because either it is a time-consuming process or it lacks political visibility, or because other efforts (such as legislative activity) produce greater political rewards. According to Ogul and other scholars in this field,[24] the most relevant factors that affect the frequency and effectiveness of legislative oversight in the United States can be summarized in the way that is outlined in table 1.1.

Committees play a significant role in defining the extent of the oversight process. Because the committee system is central to the operations of the U.S. Congress, the structure and prestige of a particular committee—as well as the support given to oversight activities by its chair—can make a difference as to whether or not the committee, or Congress itself, promotes the review of a particular issue, government agency, or piece of legislation.

Table 1.1

Factors Affecting Legislative Oversight in the United States

Structural Factors/ Institutional Level	Motivational Factors/ Individual Level
• Legal authority	• Legislators' goals:
• Staff resources	— Reelection
	— Higher office
• Committee structure	— Good policy
• Committee prestige and status	• Party affiliation/partisanship
• Visibility of issue at hand	• Committee chair support

APPLICATION OF STUDIES OF THE U.S. CONGRESS TO THE MEXICAN CASE

Despite the abundance and proliferation of studies of the U.S. Congress, they may not be readily applicable to studies of legislatures in other countries, because the U.S. Congress displays certain characteristics that are not easily reproducible in other legislative bodies: unlimited reelection, a two-party system, weak national parties in comparison to congressional parties, low party discipline, and a strong committee system. But what about countries like Mexico that have strong political parties that play a decisive role in selecting candidates for office? What about systems in which party discipline is high? What about countries in which legislators are elected by proportional representation rather than—or simultaneously with—plurality, as in Mexico?[25] If American theories are to claim universal validity, patterns of behavior that prevail in the United States must be tested in other countries. Therefore, one objective of this study is to explore the usefulness of some ideas propounded in American legislative studies in analyzing legislative oversight in Mexico.

The most relevant difference between legislatures in the United States and Mexico lies in the assumption made in American studies that legislators are driven by the possibility of reelection. However, because reelection to consecutive terms of office is prohibited by the

Mexican Constitution, it might seem reasonable to dismiss the American framework as useless and unrealistic for the Mexican system.[26] One can ask whether American approaches can be applied to a Mexican Congress to which a deputy cannot be reelected.

Although most studies of the U.S. Congress begin by assuming that legislators' main incentive is reelection, further analysis reveals that legislators are, first and foremost, rational individuals seeking office; after achieving that goal, they become reelection-oriented. The rationality assumed by U.S. studies precedes and even forms the basis for the reelection assumption. Because members are rational and because reelection is possible, they are reelection-oriented. In systems that permit reelection, as in the United States, reelection-driven behavior appears to be legislators' predominant rational strategy. But in cases where there is no such option, as in Mexico, outgoing legislators will seek alternative office. That does not mean that Mexican lawmakers are irrational, but rather that inability to stand for reelection gives rise to different rational responses and patterns of career advancement on the part of Mexican legislators than those those observed among their U.S. counterparts. Therefore, American approaches *can* be applied to the Mexican case, albeit in a modified form: the assumption of the rationality of legislators applies to both countries, even though the different institutional settings create distinct patterns of behavior in each.[27]

In addition to this first observation, another comment needs to be made. From a preliminary review of table 1.1, it appears that some factors may not be as relevant to the Mexican case. For example, the committee system within the Mexican Congress does not really operate in the same way as it does in the United States, nor is it as visible or as important. Congressional committees in Mexico are usually weak, understaffed, and underfinanced; they lack even a set of stable internal rules for their operation and therefore do not constitute decisionmaking bodies within Congress. Hence, "committee structure," "committee prestige and status," and "committee chair support" are variables that are not applicable to the Mexican Congress. However, removing committee-related factors from the Mexican context leaves several relevant variables noted for the U.S. Con-

Table 1.2
Factors Affecting Legislative Oversight in Mexico

Structural Factors/ Institutional Level	Motivational Factors/ Individual Level
• Legal authority	• Deputies' goals
• Staff resources	• Nonreelectability
	• Partisan powers of the president
	• Strength of the opposition (partisanship)

gress that can also be applied to the Mexican system: legal authority, staff resources, legislators' goals (such as alternative office), and partisanship (which is measured by the strength of the opposition, that is, the share of Chamber seats held). Two other variables can be added so that the model can reflect the Mexican context more accurately:

1. Nonreelectability to consecutive terms, given the particular case of Mexico's restriction; and

2. Partisan powers of the president—that is, the informal ability Mexico's PRI presidents had to select party leadership as well as candidates for the most important elected offices—a variable that is particularly important in light of the impact that the president's leadership over the PRI had on deputies' behavior during the period of this study.

Incorporating these changes and in an attempt to be as succinct as possible, table 1.1 can be reconfigured as table 1.2.

To refine the analytical model, it is necessary to hypothesize causal relationships among the variables presented in the table and to determine whether causal links are direct or indirect, that is, whether the causal relationship operates directly or through intervening variables. This study will also assess changes in legislative oversight (the dependent variable) along two dimensions: effectiveness (how effective deputies' efforts were at detecting misbehavior and preventing it) and frequency (how often legislative oversight was conducted).

The following hypotheses (as outlined in figure 1.1) are proposed for the Mexican case:

1. Legal authority establishes the limits of what deputies can oversee and how they can oversee it. Staff resources provide legislators with the technical, legal, and financial support needed to carry out their monitoring activities. Both are "structural factors" that, depending on availability, may expand or constrain oversight possibilities. How important these factors are in relation to "motivations" remains to be seen. The hypothesis is that their impact is considered secondary as compared to deputies' motivations and goals.

2. Nonreelectability to consecutive terms decreases the frequency and effectiveness of legislative oversight in the following ways:

   — It reduces legislators' experience within the Chamber, which may have had a bearing on the effectiveness with which deputies carried out their legislative responsibilities. (This refers to *ability* rather than *will*.)

   — It alters deputies' goals. Because they were prohibited from seeking reelection, outgoing PRI deputies deferred to the president as party chief in order to get appointed to another office after their terms had expired. In turn, this "political dependency" on the chief executive constrained PRI members' incentives to oversee the administration. If reelection had been permitted, PRI deputies would have depended more on the electorate for advancing their political careers than on other sources of political support.

3. The partisan powers of the president shaped PRI deputies' behavior because of the need to appeal to the chief executive—in his role as party chief—in order to get promoted to higher office. In turn, such altered incentives reduced the frequency of legislative oversight, since oversight depends on "how rewarded it is as compared with other activities legislators can engage in." Oversight was not considered to be conducive to attaining higher office and could even have been considered an obstacle if

Figure 1.1
Analytical Framework

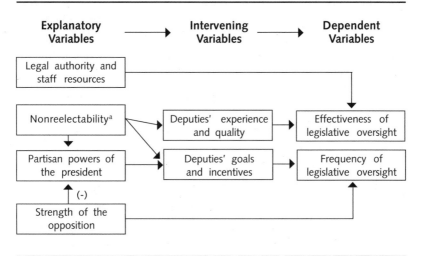

the president perceived legislative oversight as an act of defiance and disobedience to his position and authority.

4. Strength of the opposition, or partisanship, determined the frequency of oversight activities—the greater the relative size of the opposition, the more frequent the oversight. This variable also affected the president's partisan powers. As the opposition grew stronger and its members occupied more elected offices, the partisan powers of the president diminished, because there were fewer rewards and offices to offer to loyal followers. Thus, if the PRI had not enjoyed a majority, the effects of presidential partisan powers on deputies' motivations would have ceased to be relevant to the overall functioning of the Chamber.

RESEARCH METHODOLOGY

To explore the usefulness of the proposed analytical framework, and following the level of analysis suggested by studies of the U.S. Congress, it was necessary to get a glimpse of deputies' motivations, which have been shown to constitute the variable that is the most relevant to an explanation of legislative oversight in Mexico. For this reason, a series of interviews was conducted in two steps: (1) 49 in-depth interviews conducted between 1995 and 1997, and (2) a poll of 164 deputies from the 57th Legislature (1997–2000) conducted in October 1997.

The first set of in-depth interviews was conducted among individuals who either were deputies at the time of the interview or had been deputies at some time during the period under study. In an attempt to ensure truly representative responses, the sample exhibits the following important characteristics: (1) interviewees' party affiliation reflects, to some extent, the average distribution of Chamber seats among major parties between 1970 and 1997; (2) respondents include deputies from each of the nine legislatures that existed during that period; and (3) the sample includes deputies who sat on the most important congressional committees, including the two committees most relevant to legislative oversight (and to the primary focus of this study), the Budget and Supervisory Committees.

An initial questionnaire was designed to "measure" deputies' preferences for and attitudes toward various issues related both to their own motivations and to legislative oversight. With Aberbach's 1990 study (in which the author used quantitative analyses to explain legislative oversight in the U.S. Congress) as a guide,[28] a questionnaire was designed, mostly with closed questions, in which respondents were asked to indicate the intensity of their attitudes toward various aspects of legislative oversight and behavior. The questionnaire also included several open questions. To provide more statistical significance and reliability to the interview process, another questionnaire was designed in 1997; it included many of the original questions. With the assistance of polltakers from Mexico's *Reforma* newspaper, the questionnaire was administered to 164 deputies in the 57th Legislature in October 1997.[29] The questionnaire was based on closed questions in an effort to gauge the intensity of deputies' attitudes toward legislative oversight as well as their own motivations.

The chapters that follow attempt to apply and explain the analytical model outlined in this chapter. The study will first describe in detail actual instances of oversight in two areas: oversight of public spending and the formation and operation of investigative committees. A theoretical framework will then be applied to explain the possible causes of the ineffectiveness and infrequency of legislative oversight in Mexico.

Notes

[1] Alonso Lujambio, "Entre Pasado y futuro: La Ciencia política y el Poder Legislativo en México," *Estudios* 54 (Autumn 1998): 27.

[2] Rudolph de la Garza, "The Mexican Chamber of Deputies and the Mexican Political System" (Ph.D. diss., University of Arizona, 1972), p. 4.

[3] Ibid., p. 7.

[4] The principal works dealing with the history of the Mexican Congress include the following: Ignacio Burgoa, *Breve Estudio sobre el poder legislativo* (Mexico City, 1966); Marcello Carmagnani, *Estado y mercado: La Economía pública del liberalismo mexicano, 1850–1911* (Mexico City: Fondo de Cultura Económica, 1994); Daniel Cosío Villegas, *La Constitución de 1857 y sus críticos* (Mexico City, 1957); Leon Guzmán, "El Sistema de dos cámaras y sus consecuensias," *Estudios Parlamentarios* 2, no. 1 (August–November 1992) (originally published in 1870); Frank A. Knapp, *Parliamentary Government and the Mexican Constitution of 1857: A Forgotten Phase of Mexican Political History* (San Diego: Center for U.S.-Mexican Studies, University of California at San Diego, 1953); José López Portillo y Rojas, "El Congreso en el Porfiriato," in *Elevación y caída de Porfirio Díaz* (Mexico City: Editorial Miguel Angel Porrúa, 1975 [1921]); Pablo Piccato, *Congreso y revolución: Ensayo* (Mexico City: Instituto Nacional de Estudios Históricos de la Revolución Mexicana, Secretaría de Gobernación, 1991); Emilio O. Rabasa, *La Constitución y la dictadura* (Mexico City, 1912); Reynaldo Sordo, *El Congreso en la Primera República Centralista* (Mexico City: Colegio de México and Instituto Tecnológico Autónomo de México, 1993); and Zubia Torres, *La política y el Poder Legislativo* (Mexico City, 1963).

[5] Although Congress was not precisely a "parliamentary" experiment in the strict sense of the word, since the presidential system of government was still the one supported by law, the 1857 Constitution granted Congress ample powers to oversee and influence the government's actions. The historical lesson learned by subsequent constitutional lawmakers was to avoid such congressional strength because of the stalemate and deadlock that characterized those

years. In 1917, the drafters of the Constitution explicitly stated that they would vest ample powers in the executive branch in order to avoid the predominance of Congress that occurred in the nineteenth century. Ignacio Marván briefly reviewed the debate surrounding the 1857 Constitution and its effects on Congress. According to him, "the 1857 Constitution as an institutional structure aimed at organizing the functioning and stability of public powers was truly absurd: it attempted to build a presidential system starting from the basis of 'congressional supremacy'; and it sought to consolidate constitutional preeminence and the rule of law while simultaneously maintaining the 'sovereignty' of federal and state powers" (see Ignacio Marván Laborde, *Y Después del presidencialismo? Reflexiones para la formación de un nuevo régimen* [Mexico City: Editorial Océano 1997], p. 52).

[6] See Sordo, *El Congreso en la Primera República Centralista*.

[7] See Rabasa, *La Constitución y la dictadura*.

[8] Cosío Villegas, *La Constitución de 1857 y sus críticos*.

[9] Knapp, *Parliamentary Government and the Mexican Constitution of 1857*. According to Lujambio, Knapp's research is the "best analysis of the constitutional structure of 1857 and its effects on the traditionally antagonistic relationship between the executive and legislative branches under the presidencies ... of Juárez and Lordo" (see Alonso Lujambio, "Compartir el poder: Gobiernos divididos," *Reforma* [Special Supplement: *Enfoque*], May 25, 1997, p. 52).

[10] The most noteworthy studies on the topic of constitutional and legal foundations include Manuel Barquín Alvarez, "El Control del Senado sobre el Ejecutivo: Un Equilibrio oscilante de poderes," in *Estudios jurídicos en torno a la Constitución Mexicana de 1917, en su Septuagésimo Quinto Aniversario* (Mexico City: Instituto de Investigaciones Jurídicas, Universidad Nacional Autónoma de México, 1992); Manuel Barquín Alvarez, "El Control parlamentario sobre el Ejecutivo desde una perspectiva comparativa," *Revista Mexicana de Estudios Parlamentarios*, January–April 1991; Jorge Carpizo, *El Presidencialismo mexicano* (Mexico City: Siglo XXI Editores, 1978); Jesús Orozco Henríquez, "Las Legislaturas y sus funciones de control sobre la actividad gubernamental," in Senado de la Républica, *Política y proceso legislativos* (Mexico City: Universidad Nacional Autónoma de México and Editorial Miguel Angel Porrúa, 1985); José F. Ruiz Massieu, "Las Relaciones entre el Poder Ejecutivo y el Congreso de la Unión: El Trabajo legislativo, el control político y la planeación legislativa," in ibid.; Felipe Tena Ramírez, *Derecho constitucional mexicano* (Mexico City: Editorial Miguel Angel Porrúa, 1994); and Diego Valadés, "Las Relaciones de control entre el Legislativo y en Ejecutivo en México," *Revista Mexicana de Estudios Parlamentarios*, January–April 1991.

[11] Tena, *Derecho constitucional mexicano*.

[12] Carpizo, *El Presidencialismo mexicano*.

[13] Scholarly works dealing with this topic include Alberto Díaz Cayeros and Beatriz Magaloni, "Autoridad presupuestal del poder legislativo en México: Una Primera aproximación," *Política y Gobierno*, 5, no. 2 (1998): pp. 503-28; Alicia Hernández Chávez, *La Nueva Relación entre Legislativo y Ejecutivo: La Política económica 1982-1997* (Mexico City: Instituto de Investigaciones Legislativas de la Cámara de Diputados, Instituto Politécnico Nacíonal, Colegio de México and Fondo de Cultura Económica, 1998); María Mijangos Borja, "El Control del presupuesto en una democracia," in *El Poder Legislativo en la actualidad* (Mexico City: Cámara de Diputados and Universidad Nacional Autónoma de México, 1994); Ignacio Pichardo Pagaza, *Reflexiones sobre el proceso presupuestal en la Cámara de Diputados: Un Enfoque comparativo* (Mexico City: Instituto Nacional de Administración Pública, 1981); Jeffrey Weldon, "El Proceso presupuestario en México: Defendiendo el poder del bolsillo," *Perfiles Latinoamericanos* 6 (June 10, 1997); Luis Carlos Ugalde, "El Poder fiscalizador de la Cámara de Diputados en México," in *El Control de las finanzas públicas*, ed. Gilberto Rincón Gallardo (Mexico City: Centro de Estudios para la Reforma del Estado, 1996); and Luis Carlos Ugalde, "Vigilando a los gobernantes," *Reforma* (Special Supplement: *Enfoque*), July 4, 1996.

[14] The primary research on the consequences of nonconsecutive reelection has been done by Luisa A. Béjar, "La Reelección parlamentaria en México," *Asamblea* 4, no. 4 (May 1995); Emma Campos, "Un Congreso sin congresistas: La No-Reelección consecutiva en el Poder Legislativo mexicano, 1934-1997" (B.A. thesis, Instituto Tecnológico Autónomo de México, 1996); Maite Careaga, "Reformas institucionales que fracasan: El Caso de la reforma reeleccionista en el Congreso Mexicano, 1964–1965" (B.A. thesis, Instituto Tecnológico Autónomo de México, 1996); Alonso Lujambio, "La Cámara de Diputados en México: Arreglos institucionales y proceso político," in *Federalismo y Congreso*, ed. Alonso Lujambio (Mexico City: Universidad Nacional Autónoma de México, 1995); Alonso Lujambio, "Para qué Servirían las reelecciónes en México?" *Quórum*, April 1993; Alonso Lujambio, "Reelección legislativa y estabilidad democrática," *Estudios* (1992); Benito Nacif-Hernández, "The Mexican Chamber of Deputies: The Political Significance of Non-Consecutive Re-election" (Ph.D. diss., Faculty of Social Studies, Oxford University, 1995); Luis Carlos Ugalde, "El Poder fiscalizador de la Cámara de Diputados"; Luis Carlos Ugalde, "Los Aspectos legislativos del gasto público en México, 1970-96," *Perfiles Latinoamericanos* 6 (June 10, 1997); and Luis Carlos Ugalde, "Consideraciones sobre la reelección en México," *Nexos* 15 (May 1992).

[15] Michael L. Mezey, "Legislatures: Individual Purpose and Institutional Performance," *Political Science: The State of the Discipline II*, ed. Ada W. Finifter (Washington, D.C.: American Political Science Association, 1993) p. 335.

[16] See Kenneth A. Shepsle, "The Changing Textbook Congress," in *Can the Government Govern?* ed. John E Chubb and Paul E. Peterson (Washington, D.C.: The Brookings Institution, 1989).

[17] See David R. Mayhew, *Congress: The Electoral Connection* (New Haven, Conn.: Yale University Press, 1974). See also Mayhew, "The Electoral Connection and the Congress," in *Congress: Structure and Policy,* ed. Matthew D. McCubbins and Terry Sullivan (Cambridge and New York: Cambridge University Press, 1987).

[18] Mayhew, "The Electoral Connection and the Congress," p. 24. Morris Fiorina and Richard Fenno, in 1977 and 1978, respectively, provided further detail and structure to Mayhew's themes. Mezey wrote that "Fiorina explained … that legislators ensured their re-election by intervening with the bureaucracy to gain favors for the individual constituents as well as favorable treatment in the disbursement of federal funds for the constituency as a whole…. Thus as Mayhew suggested, the re-election goals of legislators had consequences for what they did in Washington." As for Fenno, Mezey explained his contribution as one that described in rich detail exactly what legislators did in regard to their constituencies: "Credit claiming, position-taking, and advertising were all apparent in Fenno's discussion of representatives constantly in touch with their constituents" (see Mezey, "Legislatures," p. 336).

[19] The literature on congressional oversight and control of the bureaucracy is varied and immense. In this study, I explore only one of the areas covered in the literature, leaving aside other important approaches and theories. For a historical and comparative review of legislative oversight approaches, see William F. West, *Controlling the Bureaucracy: Institutional Constraints in Theory and Practice* (New York: M. E. Sharpe, 1995), chap. 6.

[20] Morris Ogul, *Congress Oversees the Bureaucracy: Studies in Legislative Supervision* (Pittsburgh: University of Pittsburgh Press, 1976).

[21] Ibid., p. 11.

[22] Ibid., p. 13.

[23] Ibid., p. 17.

[24] See, for example, Fred Kaiser, "Oversight of Foreign Policy: The U.S. House Committee on International Relations," *Legislative Studies Quarterly* 2 (1977): 255–79; Alan Rosenthal, "Legislative Behavior and Legislative Oversight," *Legislative Studies Quarterly* 6 (1981): 115–31; Bert A. Rockman, "Legislative–Executive Relations and Legislative Oversight," *Legislative Studies Quarterly* 9 (1984): 387–440; and Joel D. Aberbach, *Keeping a Watchful Eye: The Politics of Congressional Oversight* (Washington, D.C.: The Brookings Institution, 1990).

[25] For instance, "in some countries with proportional representation, the link between legislators and their constituents seems weaker. In the Netherlands, for example, where there are no local constituencies and all candidates run on nationwide lists, voters say that they are unlikely to go to MPs with problems or complaints and MPs, in describing their roles, place very little emphasis on dealing with voters' problems" (see Mezey, "Legislatures," p. 341).

[26] Article 59 of the 1917 Mexican Constitution prohibits consecutive reelection but permits deputies to return to the Chamber if at least a full term intervenes. Chapter 4 of this study provides a detailed discussion.

[27] As chapter 4 will show, whereas the reelection goal of American Congress members fosters a pattern of behavior characterized by "static ambition" (in which members seek to secure a long career in office), in Mexico, the prohibition of consecutive reelection fosters a pattern of behavior that is characterized by "progressive ambition" (in which deputies are forced to seek alternative office when their terms expire).

[28] Aberbach, *Keeping a Watchful Eye.*

[29] The agreement with *Reforma* was that I would have the right to publish the results of the poll as empirical evidence for my dissertation, and that they would also have the right to publish some figures. Indeed, I wrote an article explaining some conclusions resulting from this poll (see Luis Carlos Ugalde, "Requieren asesores y reelección: Diputados de la 57 Legislatura," *Reforma,* December 16, 1997).

CHAPTER TWO

OVERSIGHT OF PUBLIC FINANCES

OVERSIGHT OF PUBLIC FINANCES IS ONE OF THE PRIMARY WAYS FOR the legislative branch to exert effective control over the government's formulation of public policy. The so-called "power of the purse" is the main tool most legislative bodies around the world use to influence public policy, to keep a watchful eye over its design and implementation, and to curb and mitigate waste and mismanagement within government organizations. In Mexico, the law grants sufficient authority to Congress to oversee public expenditures.[1] Unfortunately, that legislative authority has not been translated into an effective mechanism for influencing policymaking and curbing government corruption and mismanagement.

The Mexican Chamber of Deputies oversees public finances through a complex, multiyear budgetary process that includes approval of the budget by the Chamber as well as a review of the budget at the end of the fiscal year, after the money has been spent. Seen this way, the budgetary cycle (depicted in figure 2.1) can be divided into three stages:

1. Drafting the budget by the executive branch (Ministry of the Treasury) and its subsequent approval by the Chamber;
2. Spending the budgeted funds by executive agencies and departments, as well as by the judicial and legislative branches of government; and
3. Reviewing public expenditures, that is, monitoring how the monies were actually spent.[2]

Figure 2.1
Stages of the Budgetary Cycle

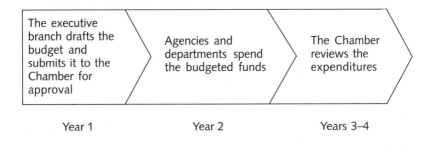

The executive branch drafts the budget and submits it to the Chamber for approval	Agencies and departments spend the budgeted funds	The Chamber reviews the expenditures
Year 1	Year 2	Years 3–4

Until 1999, the entire budgetary process took almost four years—from the time the drafting of the budget began until the Chamber concluded its oversight, audits, and investigations of public expenditures. Certain parts of the last stage went beyond that time period, however, as a result of further investigations and sanctions that required more time for completion.[3]

THE BUDGETARY PROCESS

Article 74 of the current Constitution grants the Chamber of Deputies the exclusive power "to examine, debate, and approve the annual budget of expenditures of the Federation.... The Federal Executive shall present to the Chamber ... the proposed Federal Expenditure Budget by no later than November 15 ... and the pertinent Secretary shall appear to account for [it]." The federal budget, or *Presupuesto de Egresos de la Federación* (PEF),[4] is the total sum of estimated expenses for all of the government's associated programs that are to be dispensed over each fiscal year—from January 1 to December 31—by the government units and branches listed below.

1. Legislative branch;

2. Judicial branch;

3. Executive branch:

— Office of the President,
— Ministries, administrative departments, and the Office of the Attorney General,
— Decentralized entities,
— Public enterprises (in which the state has majority participation), and
— Public trusteeships.

Drafting the Budget

In order to draft the budget bill, the Ministry of the Treasury (*Hacienda*) develops a list of criteria for the formulation of the budget for each agency and department. These guidelines contain economic policy goals, administrative procedures, and budget ceilings (if any), as well as government priorities. The manual is sent to each agency in the executive branch, to Congress, and to the judicial branch by June 15, and it serves as the basis for each agency's own blueprint or proposed budget (*anteproyecto*).[5] Each agency's *anteproyecto* contains a *Programa Operativo Anual* (POA) stating the goals to be achieved and actions to be taken during the upcoming fiscal year, as well as the particular activities to be funded by the budget. The agency's *anteproyecto* is then returned to *Hacienda* by July 20, which in turn uses the information to add up the amounts and develop a blueprint for the PEF. *Hacienda* usually requests suggestions and opinions on this first blueprint from various economic and political sources within the executive branch and, increasingly, from the legislative branch.

Once this stage is completed, the executive branch prepares the budget bill, which is normally submitted to the Chamber of Deputies in mid-November (November 15 is the deadline established by the Constitution). The PEF is sent along with the *Criterios Generales de Política Económica* (General Guidelines for Economic Policy), which consists of a general outline of economic policy for the upcoming year and a forecast of the government's primary economic targets. The finance minister presents both of these documents to the Chamber of Deputies and thereby formally inaugurates the discussion and approval process of the PEF.

This process takes approximately 4 weeks—from submission of the budget bill to the Chamber around November 15 until a vote is held in mid-December. The budget bill must be approved before the congressional session adjourns on December 15 or—when no agreement is reached—by December 31, as was the case with the 1999 budget bill, which was approved just hours before the beginning of the following fiscal year. In the years when a new administration is sworn in (as in 2000), the budget bill may be submitted by December 15 and approved by December 31. This timetable leaves an average of only 4 weeks for the Chamber to analyze and vote on the budget bill, even though this process is the most significant instance of Congress's ability to influence public policy.[6] This short period of time is in sharp contrast to the approximately 28 weeks allotted to the executive branch—which has the assistance of each department's budgeting area as well as *Hacienda's* entire bureaucracy—for drafting the budget bill.[7]

Floor Debates

As soon as the Chamber receives the budget bill, Congress members and party leaders begin issuing their opinions about the principal positive and negative aspects of the proposed budget. The budget debate frequently provides a forum for evaluating and criticizing the government's economic policy and for suggesting alternative economic models. Before the bill is voted on, floor debates take place within the Chamber, in which each party provides its evaluation of the budget bill and announces the decision of how its members will vote. Several observations can be noted from an analysis of the debates that took place between 1970 and 1997:[8]

1. Before 1982 there were very few debates. National Action Party members participated more actively than others, but their criticisms tended to be very general—only particular items were subject to criticism, not the overall design and objectives of the budget.

2. Beginning in 1983, deputies from the Left began criticizing the general orientation of the budgets, complaining that they did not provide for a socially oriented economic policy. Those

positions coincided with the economic crises that befell Mexico in the early 1980s.

3. Since the mid-1980s, the approval process for the budget—which requires the minister of the treasury to appear before the Chamber to respond to questions about the bill—has become the principal opportunity for legislators to criticize the government's economic policy, which is usually portrayed by leftist deputies as "neoliberal," "*imperialista*," and contrary to the social well-being of the Mexican population.

4. Institutional Revolutionary Party deputies have always defended the budget bill, arguing that it guarantees long-term economic stability and development. Before 1997, they would reject the opposition's proposals, claiming that they were populist in nature and that, even though they may have stimulated short-term public spending and growth, in the end, they would have proved counterproductive because of the country's inability to finance the proposed programs. As the PRI becomes an opposition party in Congress and Vicente Fox is inaugurated as chief executive, it will be interesting to observe the party's position on the new administration's economic policies. In the weeks following his electoral triumph, Fox and his team propounded the main elements of their economic program: healthy and balanced public finances, fiscal reform to increase government revenues, privatization of the power and petrochemical industries, and free trade and market reforms, among others. In essence, Fox's proposals are very similar to those of the current and previous administrations. However, in contrast to the passive support it showed in the past, the PRI announced its opposition to "neoliberal" reforms or to any other proposal to privatize state-owned industries. This ideological inconsistency may be the result of PRI legislators' past support of presidential bills out of pure party discipline and loyalty to the chief executive, or it can be attributed to PRI deputies' opposition to Fox's bills merely because he belongs to another party.

5. Opposition deputies have always criticized the short time period allowed for examination and discussion of the budget bill. The timetable gives legislators only four weeks, on average, for the arduous task of examining and discussing immense amounts of paper and data. Their criticisms became reality in the final days of 1998, when the 1999 budget bill came close to not being approved by December 31 because of the large number of controversies and changes arising from the examination of the executive branch's original submission. There was a moment during that period when many feared a constitutional crisis, because the bill lacked the consensus required for passage. Fortunately, an agreement was reached only hours before the year ended.

6. The debates over the 1999 and 2000 budget bills showed a break with the past in that—aside from the typical ideologically oriented criticisms of past debates—all the parties made more specific observations, suggested alternative strategies and goals, and presented concrete numbers to substitute for the figures provided by the government. However, the benefits of this new legislative direction are still limited because of the poor quality, inconsistency, and dubious viability of legislators' proposals, especially those made by the opposition.

Amendments

As a result of floor debates and meetings within the *Comisión de Programación y Presupuesto* (Budget Committee), parliamentary groups—especially those from the opposition—suggest amendments to the original budget bill. Even though the Constitution does not explicitly endow the Chamber with the authority to change the chief executive's proposal, there is a consensus that Congress does possess such power. The legislature has indeed exercised this power in several instances during the past decades.[9] According to Díaz and Magaloni, between 1960 and the 1980s, there were no amendments to the budget. Starting in 1982, "legislative amendments to the total amounts proposed by the executive branch began to take place; these amendments usually represented increases over the original amounts requested by the president."[10] Weldon found that, during the heyday of "metaconstitutional" presidentialism (1937–77), legislative amendments were rare; conversely, ever since the importance of metaconstitutional presidentialism has decreased (from the 1970s onward), the number of legislative amendments has increased.[11]

Although amendments have been passed since the 1980s, truly significant changes to executive proposals are evident only since 1998. As the summary of amendments presented in table 2.1 shows, before 1997, changes to the original budget proposals were limited to marginal modifications; therefore, their impact on economic policy was insignificant. By contrast, beginning in 1997, the scope and amount of amendments passed have been considerable. A case in point is the final bill approved in 1999 for the 2000 budget, which contains several significant changes to certain items in the original executive proposal: (1) a fund of $795 million (in U.S. dollars) was created by the opposition to support municipal and state governments; (2) resources available for rural development were increased by $237 million; (3) an additional $310 million was allocated to retirees; and (4) $129 million was allotted to the Secretaríat of Social Development (SEDESOL). To obtain the additional funding, the original estimated price of Mexico's oil exports was increased from $15.50 per barrel to $16; the budget for the Federal Judicial Council was reduced by $100 million; and the budget for the state-owned Mexican Petroleum Company (PEMEX) was cut by $3.1 billion.[12]

Voting on the Budget Bill

Once *Hacienda* agrees to introduce certain modifications and amendments, if any, to the original bill, the Budget Committee issues a detailed report (*dictamen legislativo*) that contains technical opinions about the budget's economic rationale and social impact, as well as a political opinion that expresses the committee's recommendation for either approval or rejection. Because PRI members presided over and dominated the Budget Committee until 1997, the *dictámenes* always requested approval of the budget. However, the

Table 2.1
Amendments to the Budget Bill, 1981–99 (selected years)

Year[a]	Amount of Original Expenditures	Administrative, Phrasing, or Format	Recommendation
		Modifications	
1981	No	No	Yes
1983	Decrease of Item 23 by 0.8%	Legislative branch budget is presented separately.	No
1986	Increase of: • Item 23 by 0.9% • Article 2 by 0.12% Decrease of Article 6 by 0.1%	Reclassification of budget items (Mexican Institute of Foreign Trade).	No
1988	Decrease of: • Article 2 by 9.8% • Article 4 by 2.8% • Article 6 by 6.08% • Article 7 by 15.4% Increase of Article 3 by 2.9% Changes to budgets of various public and decentralized entities	No	No
1990	Decrease of Article 2 by 0.01% Increase of Article 4 by 5.2%	Phrasing changes	No
1992	Decrease of Article 2 by 0.05% Increase of Article 4 by 17.5%	Format changes. Reclassification of legislative branch and IFE budgets.	No
1994	No	Phrasing changes.	Increase in legislative branch budget.

Continued

Table 2.1
Continued

		Modifications	
Year[a]	Amount of Original Expenditures	Administrative, Phrasing, or Format	Recommendation
1996	No	Phrasing changes.	No
1997	Decrease of: • 6.4 billion pesos to Fobaproa (bank bailout program) • 2.0 billion pesos to communications programs • 100 million pesos to the president's *partida secreta* • 400 million pesos to the Electoral Court Increase of 15 billion pesos to the funds of local governments	Phrasing changes. Reclassification of the social development chapter.	Privatization of the state-owned newspaper *El Nacional.* Privatization of the state-owned paper company, *Pipsa.* Regulation of salaries and bonuses of high-level public officials.
1999	Decrease of: • $100 million for the Federal Judicial Council • $3.1 billion to PEMEX Increase of: • $795 million for states and municipalities • $237 million for SAGAR, agricultural commercial development, and the rural sector • $310 million for retirees • $129 million for SEDESOL	Establishment of several obligations and requirements from SHCP, SECODAM, and other secretaríats to provide information on spending, to publish periodic reports, and to respond to variations in spending, among others.	The decree makes several recommendations to the executive branch.

[a] Year in which the budget for the upcoming fiscal year is approved.

Sources: Diary of Debates, 1981–99; various national newspapers, 1997 and 1999 (see bibliography).

growth in the opposition's presence within both the Chamber and the Budget Committee over the last decade produced a concomitant increase in disagreements with and criticisms of *dictámenes* that were favorable to the government's budget bills and economic positions. In 1997, for example, with the election of an opposition member as chair of the Budget Committee, the *dictamen* of the 1998 budget bill was approved only after the inclusion of several amendments and changes.[13]

Dictámenes are then distributed to every Congress member in an effort to guide his or her vote by providing a supposedly technical and knowledgeable opinion, after which the bill—with the amendments agreed upon between *Hacienda* and the Chamber—is finally submitted to a floor vote. Between 1970 and 1997, the House always approved the budget bill. Over that period, the budget was passed seven times by an average of 85 percent of the Chamber's vote, with a variation ranging from 60 percent—the lowest approval vote occurring in 1988—to 100 percent. From 1970 to 1979, there was a pattern of almost unanimous approval. Thereafter, a turning point is evident, showing increasing resistance to the budget bill, a shift that, not surprisingly, coincided with the opposition's larger presence within the Chamber. Although no records exist to show how individual legislators voted, a plausible hypothesis—based on the available data—suggests that the budget bill was voted on along party lines: the PRI voted in favor of the bill, while the opposition usually voted against it. This conclusion is supported by the fact that, as the presence of the opposition increased within the Chamber, especially since 1979, the percentage of votes rejecting the budget also increased (the correlation between both sets of data is 0.75 for the entire period).[14]

Nevertheless, a change in this voting pattern can be observed since 1998. For example, in 1998, 73 percent of the House voted to approve the *dictamen* of the 1999 budget bill. This is a rather large number, given the opposition's control of 52 percent of the Chamber seats at the time. The vote to approve the 2000 budget bill was even more startling: 96 percent of the deputies approved the bill. Table 2.2 presents a breakdown of the vote for selected years.

Table 2.2
Chamber Voting on the Federal Budget, 1970–99 (selected years)

Year[a]	Quorum as Percentage of Chamber's Size[b]	Percentage of Votes in Favor[c]	Percentage of Votes Against[c]	Presence of Opposition Within Chamber (%)
1970	68	100	0	16
1972	70	90	10	16
1974	75	100	0	18
1976	90	100	0	18
1978	83	100	0	18
1980	78	79	21	25
1982	83	77	23	26
1984	61	97	3	26
1986	74	75	25	28
1988	84	60	40	48
1990	76	65	35	48
1992	70	80	20	36
1993	77	76	24	36
1997	94	68	26	52
1998	93	73	27	52
1999[d]	97	96	2	52

Notes: Percentages are rounded to the nearest whole number.
[a] Year the budget vote took place. The budget was to be implemented the following year.
[b] The size of the Chamber has varied in the most recent legislatures; for example, in 1970, the Chamber membership was 213, today it is 500.
[c] Percentage with respect to Chamber's quorum on the day of the vote.
[d] Reflects the general vote.
Sources: Information obtained from the *Diary of Debates*, 1970–99. For data regarding the presence of the opposition over the period 1970–79, see Juan Molinar Horcasitas, *El tiempo de la legitimidad: Elecciones, autoritarismo y democracia en México* (Mexico City: Cal y Arena, 1991), p. 82.

In order to understand this change in voting patterns within the framework of a divided government, it is necessary to take into account the new dynamics of bargaining and negotiation that arose within the Budget Committee. Before 1997, PRI members had always chaired that committee; therefore, the committee's *dictámenes* mainly reflected the preferences of the executive branch and its party and dismissed the demands of the opposition, thereby resulting in the opposition's systematic vote against the budget bill. Ever since 1997, when a member of the opposition began to chair this committee, the drafting of *dictámenes* has become a process that involves comprehensive and difficult negotiations among *Hacienda* officials, legislators, party leaders, and even the president of the republic along with the minister of the interior—a situation that was unimaginable only a few years ago. The process resulted in substantial modifications to the original proposals sent by the executive branch before the bills were put to a vote. Consequently, because the final *dictámenes* already included significant changes reflecting the opposition's opinions, they were approved by higher percentages of the House. For example, the 96 percent vote approving the 2000 budget bill was possible only after government officials and PRI leaders accepted various amendments to the original bill. It remains to be seen how the PRI congressional delegation will vote on future budget bills, as the PRI becomes an opposition party, and the extent to which the PAN will support the budget proposal that the president submits.

LEGAL CONTROVERSIES

In addition to the legal controversy surrounding the Chamber's authority to amend executive bills, other controversies arose, which need to be clarified as well. The first refers to a legal solution to the Chamber's inability to approve the budget bill before the beginning of the fiscal year on January 1. As became evident during the last weeks of 1998 and 1999, the Constitution has no explicit provision addressing this situation. Article 74 establishes only that the Chamber has the power to "annually examine, discuss, and approve the federal budget"; it does not include the verb "reject." A cursory reading of this article would suggest that the Chamber is preempted from rejecting the budget bill submitted by the executive branch. Nevertheless, as Mijangos has pointed out, "the power to approve would lack any meaning if the power to reject did not accompany it.... If one maintains that the Chamber can approve, examine, and discuss, but cannot reject or amend, then one is reduced to the absurdity of bestowing upon the Chamber of Deputies a mechanical authority completely unrelated to the power of controlling the executive."[15] According to José Luis Soberanes, former director of the Juridical Research Institute at the National Autonomous University of Mexico, "there is a legal vacuum in budgetary legislation.... It is not clear what can be done in case a budget has not been approved by January 1.... The only thing established in the law is that public servants' salaries are to be paid on time, but no other public expenditure may be disbursed.... In such a situation, it is unclear what to do.... The president could probably initiate a constitutional controversy suit before the Supreme Court in order to solve the paralysis."[16] For Mijangos, one solution entailed "extending the preceding year's budget and adding to it the Central Bank's inflation rate.... Currently the only thing that is guaranteed, in compliance with Article 75, is payment to federal government employees."[17]

The second legal controversy refers to the president's veto power over legislative amendments to the budget bill. A strict legal interpretation suggests that this veto was not contemplated by the framers of the Constitution, because Article 72 grants the president the power to veto only laws that emanate from Congress as a whole. Given that the budget is a decree passed by only one chamber, it is not considered a law and thus cannot be subject to presidential veto.[18] However, section j of Article 72 specifically lists the cases in which a presidential veto does not apply (electoral and jury duties, criminal accusations against high-ranking officials, and convocations of extraordinary sessions of the *Comisión Permanente*). It is therefore logical to assume that, because the Constitution does not explicitly mention the budget as a case over which a veto cannot be exercised, then, according to Mijangos, the president can veto legislative amendments to the proposed budget bill.[19] Weldon argued that, legal interpretations aside, presidential vetoes have already taken place on several occasions: between 1917 and 1933, there were 42 presidential vetoes, many of them of specific items.[20] It is up to the Supreme Court or constitutional reforms enacted by the legislative branch to resolve this dispute.

The third legal controversy involves the Constitution's exclusion of the Senate from the budget approval process. The Senate is only allowed to intervene in the review and approval of revenues.[21] It should be noted that this separation of legislative jurisdiction over the budgetary process did not exist in the first Constitution of independent Mexico (1824), which gave both the upper and lower houses of Congress the authority to approve federal budgets. The situation began to change when Congress became unicameral as a result of a resolution established in the 1857 Constitution that abrogated the Senate, even though that congressional structure lasted only 17 years. Indeed, a new set of constitutional reforms reestablished the Senate and the bicameral system in 1874, but with that reform, the Senate lost its authority to participate in the budgetary process; the review and approval of the budget became an "exclusive power" of the Chamber of Deputies. That provision was ratified in the 1917 Constitution, and it has remained unaltered since that time.[22]

The lower chamber's exclusive power in budgetary matters does not seem to be based on strong historical, legal, or political arguments. Consequently, its adequacy has been criticized on several grounds.[23] First, it seems inappropriate that the Senate is allowed to intervene in the revenue approval process but is precluded from participating in its counterpart, the budgetary process. The artificial separation of the budgetary process into a revenue law and an expenditure decree has been criticized because common sense suggests that the entire process should form just one piece of legislation, which is subject to the approval of both chambers. According to Mijangos, "revenue cannot be understood without expenditures and vice versa, because we are dealing with an articulated whole where the approval process should be one and the same."[24] Second, those who argue in favor of including the Senate in the budgetary approval process claim that it is absurd for the upper chamber to be denied participation in the approval of the budget but be granted authority to participate in any modifications made to the budget bill after it has been approved.[25] In Tena's opinion, it is highly contradictory that the approval of expenditures for the whole year is the sole prerogative of the lower chamber, while the approval of subsequent spending changes falls under the jurisdiction of both chambers.[26] A third argument in favor of including the Senate in the budgetary process is based on the fact that this body represents the federal union and therefore should play a pivotal role in encouraging fiscal federalism and guaranteeing fiscal balance between the central government and the states. Finally, it can be argued that, in the case of a divided government, Senate participation in the budgetary process in Mexico could create a moderating force vis-à-vis eventual "excesses" by the Chamber of Deputies.[27]

Given the change in the dynamics between the executive and legislative branches produced by the experience of divided government, legal uncertainties surrounding the budgetary process create a potential for stalemate and confrontation between both branches of government. Until now, there have been only legal or commonsense interpretations of what can or should be done in case of deadlock or impasse. Consequently, it is imperative to modify the institutional framework to enable it to produce certainty in legal interpretations and to provide explicit solutions to all these controversies.

REVIEW OF PUBLIC EXPENDITURES:
THE *CONTADURÍA MAYOR DE HACIENDA*

After the budget bill has been approved (the first stage), and the budget has been implemented by executive agencies and departments (the second stage, which is not discussed here), the third stage of the budgetary process begins. This stage consists of the oversight of public expenditures and the review of the legality, efficiency, and effectiveness of the implementation of public programs. To perform this immense and complex task, the Chamber delegated authority to a technical body called *Contaduría Mayor de Hacienda* (Treasury Accounting Office, CMH). Until 1999, the CMH was the auditing agency of the Chamber of Deputies, and its task was to assist legislators in the oversight and review of government spending. As of 2000, as a result of constitutional reforms passed in 1999, the CMH will be replaced by the *Auditoría Superior de la Federación* (Federal Auditing Office, ASF). Although the goals and duties of the ASF will closely resemble those of the CMH, its powers and the range of entities it will supervise will be greater.[28]

Legal Powers and Resources

The Mexican Constitution confers upon Congress the power to oversee government expenditures and to control federal agencies by examining and auditing their accounts and finances. Until 1999, the *Contaduría* had oversight power over the legislative, judicial, and executive branches of government (including decentralized agencies, public trusteeships, and enterprises with majority participation by the state[29]), as well as over several areas in the private sector (including enterprises and organizations that enter into contracts with government agencies as well as those that receive federal government subsidies).

According to Article 3 of the *Contaduría*'s Federal Law, the main powers of this auditing agency (which are valid until the changes proposed in the bylaw are approved, as explained in note 28) include the following:

1. To verify that the federal government's operations, programs, and activities comply with existing regulations and related laws;[30]

2. To examine if the federal government's expenditures and investment projects are carried out in accordance with the approved budget;

3. To analyze the use and application of federal subsidies and government transfers granted to public and private entities;

4. To assess the implementation of the government's main policies and programs, as well as the degree of efficacy and efficiency in fulfilling them;

5. To promote, before competent authorities, the prosecution of allegedly culpable public officials, for either administrative or penal offenses (discussed in the next section); and

6. In carrying out its oversight responsibilities, to conduct on-site investigations, request written information, review official

Table 2.3
Number of *Contaduría* Employees, 1970–2000 (selected years)

Year	Employees
1970	279
1975	279
1981	570
1984	964
1988	1,078
1995	1,153
1997	1,210
2000	1,335

Sources: Mexico Department of the Treasury, General Accounting Office; and Leobardo J. Mendoza, "La Fiscalización de la administración pública en México" (M.A. thesis, Facultad Latinoamericana de Ciencias Sociales, 1996), p. 171.

documents, conduct audits, and hold interviews and hearings with public functionaries; if access to information is restricted or audits and on-site investigations are impeded, to report this to the Chamber of Deputies, which then decides what measures to take to rectify the situation.

To fulfill its mandate, in 1997, for example, the *Contaduría* had approximately 1,200 employees on its payroll, including secretaries, clerks, auditors, and directors. Personal interviews with members of the office indicate that this was considered a very small number, given all of the *Contaduría*'s tasks and responsibilities, which in 1997 alone included 726 audits and investigations. That figure contrasts, for example, with the 3,000 employees of the U.S. General Accounting Office, whose functions and responsibilities are similar.[31] (Table 2.3 shows the number of *Contaduría* employees for selected years.) In addition to its traditional role of advising on legal issues, systems, and administration, the *Contaduria* has specific tasks, which are reflected in its internal organization by functional area, including sections that review government revenues, government expenditures, public enterprises, public works, and programs. The structure of the agency is represented in figure 2.2.

Profile of *Contadores Mayores de Hacienda*, 1970–2001

As the organizational chart shows, the *Contaduría* is headed by a *contador mayor*, or auditor general. According to its Federal Law, the *contador mayor* is designated by the Chamber of Deputies, based on a list proposed by the Chamber's Supervisory Committee. The *contador mayor* serves an eight-year term, which is renewable only by special petition of the Supervisory Committee. The auditor general cannot be removed during the term of office, except under special circumstances under which the Supervisory Committee can recommend dismissal to the Chamber, which has final authority to vote and remove the *contador mayor*. These special circumstances include dishonesty, notorious inefficiency, physical or mental incapacity, or the intentional perpetration of a crime or offense.[32]

Between 1970 and 2000, there have been 10 auditor generals. A brief examination of their biographies and results of their work in the *Contaduría* leads to several observations that are worth noting:

1. All *contadores mayores* were "outsiders" at the time of their appointment. Since the *Contaduría* lacked a civil service structure, none of the auditor generals had worked or served within the agency. Many of them did have professional experience in areas related to financial and oversight issues, however, as was the case of Javier Castillo Ayala (1990–98), who had worked in the financial sector of the government for several years before joining the *Contaduría*.

2. Prior to their appointment as *contadores mayores*, most had had political careers linked to the PRI and to the administration.

3. The most notorious case of "political allegiance" to the administration is that of Javier Castillo Ayala, whose tenure ended in December 1998, and who had held various high-level positions in the Ministries of Budget and Treasury. When former President Carlos Salinas was budget minister in 1982–87, Castillo Ayala was his undersecretary for two years. In 1990, during

Figure 2.2
Contaduría Mayor de Hacienda: Organizational Chart

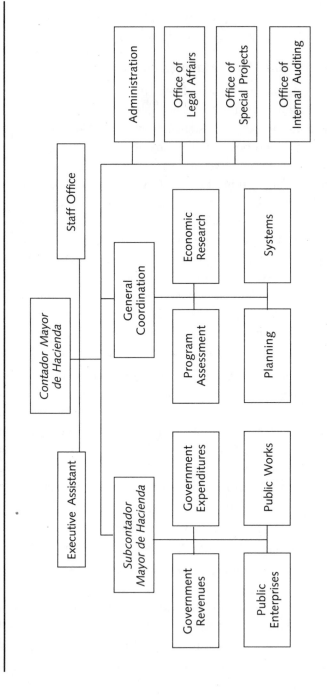

Source: Cámara de Diputados, *La Contaduría Mayor de Hacienda* (Mexico City, n.d.), p. 22.

Salinas's presidency, Castillo Ayala was selected as *contador mayor*.[33] After he left the CMH in December 1998, President Zedillo immediately appointed him undersecretary of labor.

4. Except for two auditor generals, none of the others held office for more than three years. Although the 1978 CMH Federal Law establishes a fixed term of eight years, the first auditor general under the new provisions—Francisco Rodríguez—was in office for less than two years; his successor, Enrique Ojeda, served for three years.

5. Contrary to what was intended, the post of *contador mayor* has not been relevant politically, as reflected by the fact that various *contadores mayores* left office to accept other political positions that appear to be less influential and less important. For example, Francisco Rodríguez left the office in 1979 to run (successfully) for Congress; Enrique Ojeda resigned in 1982 to return to his consulting profession; and Rodolfo González became an adviser and a mid-level official in various ministries after leaving office in 1978.[34]

6. In general, the post of *contador mayor* has not enjoyed professional or political prestige. Highly qualified and competent individuals are recruited into the executive branch, whereas *contadores mayores* have seldom been "prominent," either before or after their terms in office.[35] With the appointment of Javier Castillo Ayala in 1990, and especially that of Gregorio Guerrero in 1998, the recruiting patterns for the position have begun to change.

Table 2-4 presents brief profiles (where available) of all the auditor generals who have served through the present.

STAGES OF THE *CONTADURÍA*'S OVERSIGHT PROCESS, 1970–99

Each year, the Ministry of the Treasury publishes the previous fiscal year's Public Account, the official record listing all the financial operations and accounting records of executive branch offices. The Public Account is submitted to the Chamber and to the *Contaduría*,

Table 2.4
Contadores Mayores de Hacienda, 1970–99

Name	Term in Office	Profile
Rodolfo Merbrilla	1970–72	Not available
Antonio Lomelí	1972–73	Not available
Claudio Aponte	1973	Not available
Jesús Castillo	1973–76	Not available
Rodolfo González	1977–78	Born 1931. Engineer. Graduate studies in U.S.A. Member of the PRI. Before and after his term in office served in various ministries in mid-level and advisory positions in areas related to informational and computing systems.
Francisco Rodríguez	1978–79	Born 1911. Lawyer. Official within the PRI bureaucracy. Congress member on three occasions, one of them just after his term in office. Served in the state government of Jalisco.
Enrique Ojeda	1979–82	Not available
Miguel Rico	1982–90	Accountant. Served in the Central Bank and the Ministry of the Treasury. Undersecretary of budget in 1977.
Javier Castillo Ayala	1990–98	Born 1945. Economist. Member of the PRI. High-level positions in the Ministries of the Treasury and Budget. Undersecretary of budget when Carlos Salinas was secretary.
Gregorio Guerrero	1998–2001*	Born 1947. Accountant. Treasurer of the Chamber of Deputies before being elected *contador mayor*. Worked in various government agencies on issues related to financial operations and accounting. Does not belong to any political party.

*Because this is a transition period, the first term is for only three years; after it expires, the term can be ratified for a full period of eight years.

Sources: *Diary of Debates*, various years; *Diccionario biográfico del gobierno mexicano*, various years; several newspapers, various years.

and a review of the information constitutes the starting point of a new oversight cycle that, until 1999, had taken approximately 15 months to complete.[36]

Preliminary Stage

Before the new *Auditoría Superior de la Federación* was created, the *Contaduría* received the Public Account from the Ministry of the Treasury—via the Budget Committee—by June 10 following the end of the fiscal year. After the agency reviewed the Public Account, the *Contaduría* prepared a Preliminary Report of the Public Account (*Informe Previo*), which provided general opinions based on a preliminary review of the government's Public Account, and sent its report to the Chamber of Deputies—again by way of the Budget Committee—by November 10 following the end of the fiscal year. Based on this preliminary report, as well as its own analysis, the House Budget Committee prepared a detailed *dictamen legislativo* of the Public Account for the previous fiscal year and submitted it to the House for discussion in November. The *dictamen* served as the basis for the debate of the Public Account, which was then submitted to a floor vote.[37]

Like the budget bill, between 1970 and 1998 the Public Account was always approved by the House—by an average of 81 percent of the vote (with 65 percent being the lowest vote in 1995). The pattern of voting suggests that Congress voted on the Public Account on a partisan basis: the larger the presence of the opposition, the more votes against the report (the correlation is 0.9). (Table 2.5 summarizes the voting patterns between 1970 and 1998.) However, in 1998, a historic 98 percent of the vote approved the *dictamen,* which seems to contradict the working hypothesis in this book, because that year the opposition controlled 52 percent of the Chamber seats. A likely explanation for this seeming contradiction is that the almost unanimous approval was the result of the inclusion of the opposition's opinions in the committee's *dictámenes of the* Public Account, which, in turn, was brought about by the fact that, during that legislative session the Budget Committee was chaired by a member of the Democratic Revolutionary Party (PRD), Ricardo García Sainz.

Table 2.5
Chamber Voting on the Public Account, 1970–98 (selected years)

Year[a]	Quorum as Percentage of Chamber's Size[b]	Percentage of Votes in Favor[c]	Percentage of Votes Against[c]	Presence of Opposition Within Chamber (%)
1970	84	90	10	16
1972	69	92	8	16
1974	69	89	11	18
1976	73	91	9	18
1978	74	91	9	18
1980	79	84	16	25
1982	88	80	20	26
1985	77	81	19	28
1987	66	83	17	28
1989	68	65	35	48
1990	64	77	23	48
1992	77	74	26	36
1993	59	73	27	36
1994	74	67	33	40
1995	79	65	35	40
1998	90	98	2	52

Notes: Percentages are rounded to the nearest whole number.

[a] Year in which voting on the Public Account (corresponding to the previous year) took place.

[b] The size of the Chamber has varied over the most recent legislatures; for example, in 1970, the Chamber membership was 213, today it is 500.

[c] Percentage with respect to the Chamber's quorum on the day of the vote.

Sources: Information obtained from the *Diary of Debates*, 1970–99. For data regarding the presence of the opposition over the period 1970–79, see Molinar Horcasitas, *El tiempo de la legitimidad,* p. 82.

Investigative Stage

After completing the preliminary stage, the *Contaduría* began to collect firsthand information to verify the accuracy of the data contained in the Public Account. To do so the office conducted audits and on-site investigations, reviewed documents, and held interviews and hearings with officials of the offices being overseen. With all this new information, the CMH produced the Final Report of the Public Account (*Informe de Resultados*), which described any irregularities, illegal activities, mismanagement practices, or deviations from the original budget that were found in the course of the investigation. The Final Report was submitted to the House, by way of the Chamber's Supervisory Committee, by September 10 of the year following receipt of the Public Account—almost two years after the end of the fiscal year. To shorten this long period, the Mexican Congress recently approved a set of constitutional reforms that require the *Contaduría* to submit its Final Report to the Chamber by March 31—almost six months ahead of the schedule in effect until 1999.[38]

Sanctioning Stage

In cases where there was a presumption of wrongdoing, the *Contaduría* sent *Pliegos de Observaciones* (Notifications), which were based on its Final Report, to the public and private entities in question. In these cases, the following rules and procedures were set in motion:

1. Notified entities had 45 days to respond to the *Pliegos de Observaciones*. If they accepted the charges, they were required to name the culpable officials involved and report on the type of sanctions imposed on them. A promise to repay missing funds, if any, was usually made. If the parties denied the charges, they were obliged to provide documents and evidence to prove their innocence.

2. If responses were not received within this 45-day period, responsible officials within each entity were fined; civil servants were sanctioned by being temporarily suspended from work.

3. If the *Pliegos de Observaciones* were not invalidated or disproved by the pertinent parties, three main courses of action could be followed: the *Contaduría* could require repayment of missing funds through fiscal credits; request that "administrative" sanctions be enforced by the comptroller general's office;

or, in the case of penal offenses, present formal accusations to the attorney general.

4. Whenever top officials—ministers, heads of administrative and decentralized agencies, and directors of public enterprises— were presumed to be involved in irregularities or mismanagement practices, the individuals were prosecuted according to Title 4 of the Constitution, which delineates the responsibilities of public officials.[39]

Reviewing this complex process exposes two significant legal deficiencies that loomed as major obstacles to a more expeditious way of sanctioning functionaries and deterring corruption.[40] First, the *Contaduría* published its Final Report on the fiscal year 18 months after the year had ended. After the report was made public, the prosecution began and could take several years before reaching a conclusion. This delay in the review of public expenditures made oversight less effective and less efficient and made it difficult to apply sanctions. The new auditing body, the ASF, will expedite the oversight process by shortening the supervisory steps by 5 months. In addition, the new legislation will require government agencies and supervised public entities to submit a Progress Report of Financial Performance (*Informe de Avance de Gestión Financiera*)—covering January 1 through June 30 of the fiscal year in progress—by August 31 of that year. The opportunity for the new auditing body to detect irregularities in a timely fashion and to exert adequate controls will thus be enhanced considerably.

The second shortcoming was that the *Contaduría* did not have legal standing to directly sanction and prosecute those found guilty of corruption, illegal activities, or mismanagement. To apply sanctions, the *Contaduría* had to request legal action from various executive authorities: the attorney general, the comptroller general, and the minister of the treasury, all of whom were political appointees of the president of the republic—precisely the head of the branch that was being overseen and sanctioned. Therefore, this indirect way of imposing sanctions limited the authority of the *Contaduría* and made sanctions a bureaucratic process that was frequently blocked by political interests and groups within the executive branch.

Figure 2.3 summarizes the entire budgetary cycle described in the previous sections—drafting, approval, exercise, and oversight of public expenditures.

EVALUATION OF THE ACTUAL PERFORMANCE OF THE *CONTADURÍA*

Two general standards can be used to evaluate the performance of the *Contaduría*. On the one hand, one can try to determine if the *Contaduría* met its ultimate goal of curbing corruption and mitigating mismanagement practices in the public sector. On the other hand, one can review the internal functioning of the office (its administrative procedures and auditing operations)—as well as the rate at which the *Contaduría* sanctioned dishonest and incapable public officials—as evidence of the auditing agency's effectiveness in fighting government waste and corruption. On the first criterion—how much the *Contaduría* helped to reduce or prevent corruption—it is difficult to establish a causal relationship between observed corruption and the role the *Contaduría* played in allowing it to continue because of the agency's slow or inadequate action. In other words, it is almost impossible, at least from a methodological standpoint, to establish a causal relationship between the nonexistence of corruption—in a particular agency, for example—and a hypothesized influence of the *Contaduría* in preventing this type of behavior.

Corruption and mismanagement have been widespread in Mexico over the last decades; and the country has suffered from fraud, bankruptcy of several public enterprises, illicit enrichment of several public officials and politicians, and recurrent economic crises, among other problems. The evidence is out there. On strictly methodological grounds, however, it would be controversial to blame the *Contaduría*'s poor performance for the existence of these problems.[41] Given the difficulty of using actual corruption (or lack of it) to gauge the results of the *Contaduría*'s work, an analysis of its procedures and the sanctions it imposed can provide an indicator of the effectiveness of the *Contaduría Mayor de Hacienda*.[42]

Figure 2.3
Budgetary Cycle

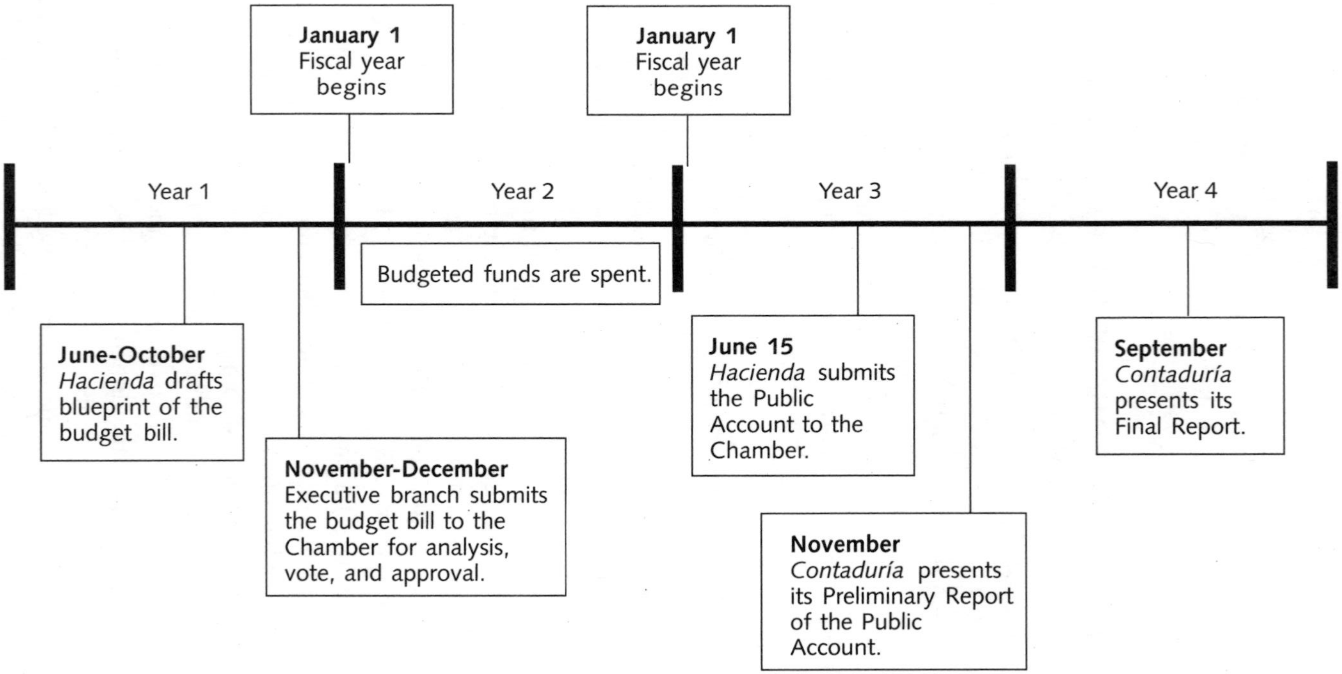

Year 1

June–October
Hacienda drafts blueprint of the budget bill.

Year 2

January 1
Fiscal year begins

November–December
Executive branch submits the budget bill to the Chamber for analysis, vote, and approval.

Budgeted funds are spent.

January 1
Fiscal year begins

Year 3

June 15
Hacienda submits the Public Account to the Chamber.

November
Contaduría presents its Preliminary Report of the Public Account.

Year 4

September
Contaduría presents its Final Report.

Sanctions

To review public spending, between 1975 and 1988, the CMH conducted 2,800 audits of more than 400 agencies in the public sector. Each audit generates various results—6 on average—therefore, approximately 17,000 results potentially contain indicators of anomalies existing in that period. In these cases, the *Contaduría*'s work produced the following results:[43]

1. In 92 cases, missing funds were repaid;

2. In 89 cases, records and proceedings were sent to the Comptroller General's Office for initiation of legal action against suspected public officials; and

3. In 76 cases, lawsuits were presented.

Adding up these cases, there were 257 instances that resulted in some sort of action, a figure that must be compared with the 2,800 audits conducted over the period and with the 17,000 results obtained from those reviews. Indeed, that low sanctioning rate— 1.5 percent in terms of results and 9 percent in terms of audits conducted—might be a reflection of the low incidence of corruption and mismanagement practices within the Mexican government. Yet, as evidence has abundantly demonstrated in recent decades, that conclusion would be far from reality. Consequently, it is plausible to argue that the low rate of legal actions initiated by the *Contaduría* really reflects its weak performance at detecting and punishing government corruption.

Recommendations

Each year, based on its audits as well as its on-site investigations, the *Contaduría* made hundreds of recommendations to government agencies in an attempt to increase efficiency, curb wasteful procedures, and improve performance. By law, public agencies were required to respond to and implement these recommendations, but the evidence suggests a low rate of compliance. According to García Villa, chair of the Supervisory Committee between 1994 and 1997, one of the best ways to evaluate the effectiveness of the *Contaduría*'s oversight is to review the attention given to its recommendations.[44]

Table 2.6
Responses to *Contaduría* Recommendations
(in percent of total)

Year	Recommendations	Partially Answered
1982	74.4	NA
1984	NA	NA
1986	43.6	6.9
1988	59.8	2.7
1990	65.8	1.8
1992	63.9	2.6

Source: Calculated by the author based on final reports of the *Contaduría Mayor de Hacienda*, several years.

The *Contaduría* scored poorly in that regard: between 1982 and 1992, for example, the average rate of response to its recommendations was 61 percent, with figures as low as 43 percent in 1986.[45] (See table 2.6.) The level of response was so low that, in 1994, the follow-up section to the recommendations was omitted from the agency's Final Report. These findings, though limited, demonstrate the poor and ineffective performance of the *Contaduría* over the period of study. Although they do not constitute scientific proof per se, the data certainly reflect a weak and inadequate job carried out by that auditing office.

Information Costs

One structural factor that limited the *Contaduría*'s effectiveness at detecting corruption was the high cost of information the office faced in its daily operation. Information costs are of several kinds: (1) costs of measuring the attributes of goods and services; (2) bargaining costs for reaching agreements and awarding contracts; (3) monitoring costs for ensuring that the terms of those contracts are fulfilled; (4) enforcement costs to guarantee that the rule of law is respected; and (5) costs to protect property rights.[46] The various information costs incurred by the *Contaduría* in performing its functions are obvious. Of particular importance were the information costs attributed to reviewing public spending, monitoring the legality of government transactions, and detecting mismanagement. These costs can be measured in terms of the resources—human, technical, and financial—needed to conduct audits and on-site investigations and to review the legality of the government's operations. Given the impossible task of overseeing every transaction and activity in the public sector, the *Contaduría* was able to oversee only a small set of agencies annually.

From 1978 to 1994, for example, the *Contaduría* was able to audit, on average, only 8.9 percent of public enterprises, which form the so-called *sector paraestatal*. And there were years—such as 1978, 1980, and 1981—during which the office audited less than 1 percent of the entities within that sector. Fortunately, the number of agencies audited and the number of audits conducted have increased steadily in the last decade. In 1978, for example, the *Contaduría* could conduct only 47 audits of 20 government agencies. As table 2.7 shows, that low figure has been increasing, and in 1997, 726 audits were conducted. Even though the number of both audits and entities audited is increasing, it is still insufficient for the purpose of obtaining an "accurate" picture of the state of affairs of government operations. In the future, more resources will be needed to improve the extent of this watchful legislative eye.

The complex nature of the subject matter examined by the *Contaduría* also increased its information costs. Records of public agencies consist of multivolume books of several hundred pages each, containing financial and technical information on very specialized and varied subjects. Frequently, the books do not follow the same, or even standard, accounting formats, making the task quite complex. At other times, information contained in some books disagrees with or even contradicts that found in other books or sources; and repeatedly the information required is either unavailable or not provided to auditors. Information costs constitute a structural constraint to the improvement of any auditing office's performance. Even though these costs are unavoidable, there are various ways to reduce them, including, among others, (1) making the law more

Table 2.7
Audits and Number of Government Entities Audited
by the *Contaduría Mayor de Hacienda*, 1978–97

| Year | Sector Central | | | Sector Paraestatal | | | Audits per Year[c] |
	Entities[a]	Audited Entities	%	Entities[b]	Audited Entities	%	
1978	20	15	75	891	5	0.5	47
1979	20	13	65	898	10	1.1	67
1980	20	5	25	903	6	0.6	23
1981	20	5	25	872	4	0.4	14
1982	20	9	45	1,155	14	1.2	185
1984	20	14	70	1,049	33	3.1	390
1986	20	12	60	737	40	5.4	391
1988	20	15	75	412	45	10.9	342
1990	20	13	65	280	57	20.3	393
1991	20	15	75	241	62	25.7	439
1992	20	17	85	217	40	18.4	500
1993	20	18	90	210	37	17.6	551
1994	20	17	85	216	47	21.7	552
1996	20	NA	NA	216	NA	NA	670
1997	20	NA	NA	216	NA	NA	726

[a] According to Articles 1 and 26 of the *Ley Orgánica de la Administración Pública Federal* (1994), the *Administración Pública Centralizada* is composed of the Office of the President, 17 ministries, the Federal District Department, and the Office of the Attorney General, which together add up to 20 entities. Although in the last 25 years there have been variations in this number—within a range of ±2, 20—is used here as a constant.

[b] According to Article 1 of the *Ley Orgánica de la Administración Pública Federal* (1994), the *Administración Pública Descentralizada* is formed mainly by decentralized entities, public enterprises, and public trusteeships.

[c] This column shows the total number of audits conducted each year by the *Contaduría*, an amount that is greater than the sum of the audited entities of both the *sector central* and the *sector paraestatal*, due to the fact that each entity usually undergoes several different kinds of audits (financial, legal, and systems, among others).

Sources: Informe Previo de la Cuenta de la Hacienda Pública Federal (Mexico City: Contaduría Mayor de Hacienda and Cámara de Diputados, 1969–93); *Informe de Resultados sobre la Revisión de la Cuenta de la Hacienda Pública Federal* (Mexico City: Contaduría Mayor de Hacienda and Cámara de Diputados,1969–93). For the number of entities within the *sector paraestatal*: for 1977–81, see *Manual de Organización de la APF* (Mexico City: Presidencia de la República, 1982); for 1982–94, see *El proceso de enajenación de entidades paraestatales* (Mexico City: Unidad de Desincorporación de Entidades Paraestatales de la Secretaría de Hacienda y Crédito Público, 1994).

explicit as regards the responsibilities of public agencies to provide information in a timely manner, (2) reorganizing the *Contaduría* internally to pursue economies of scale in its daily operations, (3) introducing new technologies to monitor government operations, and (4) improving accounting procedures throughout the federal government.

THE SUPERVISORY COMMITTEE

Until 1999, the Supervisory Committee was the only Chamber committee whose existence was recognized by the Constitution (Article 74, section 2). Legislation passed in 1999 creating the ASF took away the Supervisory Committee's constitutional standing but increased its authority and resources. The committee's continued existence will be guaranteed by federal legislation (*Ley de Fiscalización Superior de la Federación*).[47] Until 1999, the Supervisory Committee had the following powers:

1. To act as the means of communication and the official link between the *Contaduría* and the Chamber of Deputies;

2. To review the annual budget of the *Contaduría* and submit it to the Chamber for approval;

3. To issue the *Contaduría*'s bylaws;

4. To order the *Contaduría* to conduct audits and on-site investigations of certain entities that, according to the committee, required further examination;

5. To submit to the Chamber a list of candidates for the post of *contador mayor*, from which the head of the *Contaduría* was appointed;

6. To provide, when necessary, a legal interpretation of the *Contaduría*'s Federal Law and bylaws and to resolve controversies over their application, if any; and

7. To make recommendations and to order corrective actions that would guarantee the fulfillment of the *Contaduría*'s tasks and responsibilities.

It is obvious that the Supervisory Committee's main function was to ensure that the *Contaduría*'s oversight responsibilities were carried out adequately and efficiently—that is, the committee was charged with monitoring the monitor. Like the *Contaduría*'s work, the Supervisory Committee's oversight performance was quite poor over most of the period of study. Beginning in 1994–95, however, the committee's performance began to improve as a result of the increasing number of opposition deputies on the committee as well as its higher political visibility. Finding indicators to assess the oversight performance of the Supervisory Committee was even more difficult than it was in the case of the *Contaduría*, simply because there were almost no records at all. For example, it was surprising to discover that, as of 1995, there were no archives of meetings held or activities undertaken during previous legislative sessions. One of the two staff members of the committee reported that, upon arriving at the office in December 1994 "the office had only chairs and tables, but no files of past activities."[48] According to Javier Castillo Ayala, auditor general in 1990–98, "before 1994, members of the Supervisory Committee did not even read the reports issued by the *Contaduría*, nor did they meet on a regular basis. During 1995, for example, there were about 12 meetings, more than all the meetings held in the previous nine years. Formal and registered meetings of the Supervisory Committee began to take place only in 1992. Before that, either meetings did not occur, or they were not registered."[49]

With the election of PAN Congressman Juan A. García Villa as chair of the Supervisory Committee in 1994, the situation began to change. Members began to meet on a monthly basis, and the press began to monitor the committee's activities. The *Contaduría*'s reports started to get ample coverage in the media, and the chair of the committee became a noticeable political player as a result of his severe criticism of anomalies found in past government expenditures.

Another indicator of the Supervisory Committee's low profile and insignificant role over many decades is the number of times that the committee was mentioned during floor debates. During the period 1965–74, for example, the Supervisory Committee was mentioned only 32 times, as compared with the Treasury Committee,

Table 2.8
Relative Importance of Chamber Committees
(according to references in floor debates)

Period	Supervisory Committee	Budget Committee	Treasury Committee	*Gobernación* Committee
1965–74	32	417	1,855	1,083
1974–77	40	895	777	1,403
1977–80	158	451	611	568
1980–83	230	804	1,780	2,196
1983–86	280	757	1,734	1,459
1986–89	266	1,045	2,154	2,630
1989–91	409	1,062	2,015	2,708
1991–94	529	685	1,955	2,859
Average	**243**	**764**	**1,610**	**1,863**

Source: CD-ROM analysis of *Diary of Debates*, 1965–94.

which was mentioned 1,855 times. Even though, as table 2.8 shows, this number increased steadily between 1965 and 1994—from 32 to 529—the figures are still very low when compared with the Budget, Treasury, and *Gobernación* Committees in each period. On average, over that same period, the Supervisory Committee was referred to only 243 times—one-third of the references made to the Budget Committee, one-sixth of those made to the Treasury Committee, and one-seventh of those made to the *Gobernación* Committee.

The Supervisory Committee's low figures reflect not only its lack of visibility and significance over the period of study but also its ineffectiveness in detecting and denouncing mismanagement practices. Had the committee been more successful, surely it would have been more visible in floor debates.[50] It should be noted, however, that the legislation enacted in 1999 gives the Supervisory Committee the authority to create an Evaluation and Control Unit to supervise the performance of the newly created ASF. This additional resource will certainly increase the committee's capacity to oversee the ASF.

Finally, it is interesting to consider how supervising chains are created to oversee other supervisors and thus "guarantee" their impartiality and overall effectiveness. The new *Auditoría*—the principal supervisor of government branches—will be overseen by another supervisor, the proposed Evaluation and Control Unit, which in turn will be monitored by the Supervisory Committee. And the latter is ultimately subject to the scrutiny of the Chamber of Deputies, which, at least in theory, is overseen by the electorate and by public opinion at large.[51]

THE NEW AUDITING AGENCY:
THE *AUDITORÍA SUPERIOR DE LA FEDERACIÓN*

In 1999, the Mexican Congress approved various modifications to constitutional articles in order to establish the *Auditoría Superior de la Federación* as of January 2000. In December 1999, the Chamber of Deputies approved a proposed new supervisory law, *Ley de Fiscalización Superior de la Federación*, which was amended by the Senate in April 2000 and returned to the lower house for review and final approval (as explained in note 28 in this chapter). In the months to come, as soon as the law is enacted, the new *Auditoría* is expected to begin operating with full authority. All these new legal stipulations will help overcome the many legal and technical deficiencies that have hindered the performance of the *Contaduría Mayor de Hacienda*. Consequently, a brief summary of the most important provisions of the proposed federal supervisory law that will govern the new *Auditoría* is in order:

1. The political and management autonomy of the new auditing agency will be increased.
2. Legislative oversight will be expedited: the final audit report must be submitted on March 31 of the year following receipt of the Public Account from the executive branch, rather than on September 10, as the previous legislation required. Similarly,

supervised entities will be required to submit financial progress reports by August 31, covering the first six months of the fiscal year in progress (Articles 8, 9, and 30).

3. The scope of agencies and activities subject to supervision will be broadened. In addition to the three branches of government, the new *Auditoría* will be able to audit federal transfers to state and municipal governments, to autonomous bodies, or to any person or group that administers federal funds (Articles 4, 16, and 33).

4. The power to prosecute allegedly corrupt officials will be increased and sanctions will be made explicit in cases where authorities do not provide the information requested by the auditing agency (Articles 16, 33, 40, 45, 47, 49, 51, and 52).

5. More emphasis will be placed on audits related to the efficiency and effectiveness of government performance (Article 14).

6. The information obtained from ASF audits will clearly state that it is "public" and available for review.

7. The Supervisory Committee will be given more power and resources to monitor the ASF's performance with the creation of the Evaluation and Control Unit (Articles 67 and 92).

8. The internal organization and recruiting capabilities of the ASF will be strengthened by the establishment of civil service positions (Article 85).

In addition to the legal and technical deficiencies that impeded the *Contaduría's* performance (many of which should be overcome as a result of the proposed ASF provisions), political factors have also limited the agency's performance. Because these same factors will certainly be present to obstruct the work of the new *Auditoría*, they will be discussed in detail in later chapters in this book.

Notes

[1] See Weldon, "El Proceso presupuestario en México"; and Díaz and Magaloni, "Autoridad presupuestal del Poder Legislativo en México," pp. 503–28.

[2] See Ugalde, "Vigilando a los gobernantes."

[3] The constitutional reforms that created the *Auditoría Superior de la Federación* will compress the budgetary process by approximately five months.

[4] The budget specifies the federal government's overall expenditures in general, as well as the amount of funds to be allocated to each administrative unit to carry out its public programs in particular. In legal terms, "the budget is a legally binding document whereby the Chamber of Deputies grants spending authority to agencies of the federal government." To cover these expenditures, the budget is accompanied by a revenue bill, which "determines the financial resources derived from the collection of taxes, the selling of goods and services provided by the government, and the level of public borrowing" (see Nacif-Hernández, "The Mexican Chamber of Deputies," p. 205).

[5] See Weldon, "El Proceso presupuestario," pp. 4–7.

[6] The *Unidad de Estudios de Finanzas Públicas* (the Mexican counterpart of the U.S. Congressional Budget Office) was created in 1998 to strengthen the Chamber's independent economic analysis of budgetary and economic issues. The purpose of the new agency is to provide committees and Congress members—regardless of party affiliation—with technical expertise on issues related to public finances. The agency has a nonpartisan staff of 40, and its legal status comes from the new Organic Law of the Mexican Congress. Since its creation, the *Unidad de Estudios de Finanzas Públicas* has begun to provide support to deputies for their analysis of budget and revenue bills, as well as *Hacienda*'s quarterly economic reports.

[7] For many years, deputies from all parties have criticized the short period of time they have to analyze and vote on the budget bill. Most of them have suggested lengthening the period by requiring the executive branch to submit the budget bill weeks ahead of the current deadline of November 15. A proposal to amend the budget law, approved by the Chamber of Deputies in 1999, might partially address this problem by requiring the executive branch to submit the main aspects of the proposed budget in September, leaving November 15 as the unaltered deadline for final submission. This proposal, which still requires Senate approval for it to become a law, recognizes the need to have a longer period for discussion of the budget, but it also asserts that the extension should be legislated by means of a constitutional reform of Article 74.

[8] Cámara de Diputados. *Diario de debates* (Diary of Debates), 1969–98 (hereinafter cited as *Diary of Debates*).

[9] See María Mijangos Borja, "La Naturaleza jurídica del presupuesto," *Quórum*, September–October 1987; Díaz and Magaloni, "Autoridad presupuestal del Poder Legislativo"; and Weldon, "El Proceso presupuestario."

[10] See Diaz and Magaloni, "Autoridad presupuestal del Poder Legislativo," p. 515.

[11] For Weldon, metaconstitutional presidentialism exists when three conditions are met simultaneously: unified government, party discipline, and the recognition of the president as party leader (see Weldon, "El Proceso presupuestario," p. 2).

[12] The information was provided by Ena Victoria Rosas Medina and gathered from various interviews and press analyses. The exchange rate used to convert to dollars is the average in effect in April 2000, which was 9.5 pesos per U.S. dollar.

[13] During the 57th Legislature (1997–2000), the Budget Committee was chaired by Ricardo García Sainz of the Democratic Revolutionary Party, and the PRI no longer had a majority within that body. This new pluralism has converted the Budget Committee and the chamber floor into real arenas for bargaining and influencing the terms and conditions of the budget.

[14] The correlation coefficients for subperiods are lower: for 1979–84, $r = 0.5$; for 1985–93, $r = 0.45$.

[15] Mijangos, "La Naturaleza jurídica del presupuesto," pp. 29–30.

[16] Reported in *El Financiero*, December 14, 1997.

[17] See Mijangos, "La Naturaleza jurídica del presupuesto," p. 30.

[18] See Carpizo, *El Presidencialismo mexicano;* and Tena, *Derecho constitucional mexicano.*

[19] See Mijangos, "La Naturaleza jurídica del presupuesto," pp. 31–32.

[20] See Weldon, *El Proceso presupuestario*, pp. 17–18.

[21] See Articles 72, 73, and 74 of the 1917 Constitution.

[22] For a historical review of congressional budgetary powers, see Cámara de Diputados, *Derechos del pueblo mexicano: México a través de sus constituciones*, vol. 8 (Mexico City: Cámara de Diputados, 1994), pp. 657–773. Also see Jeffrey Weldon, "The Legal and Partisan Framework of the Legislative Delegation of the Budget in Mexico," manuscript, Instituto Tecnológico Autónomo de México, 1999.

[23] See Tena, *Derecho constitucional mexicano.* I am grateful to Ena Victoria Rosas Medina for her comments and insights, which have been reflected in this section.

[24] See Mijangos, "La Naturaleza jurídica del presupuesto," p. 28.

[25] See Amador Rodríguez Lozano, "La Reforma del estado y el Congreso de la Unión: Una Visión desde el Senado sobre el fortalecimiento del Poder Legislativo en México," *Revista del Senado de la República* 1, no. 3 (April–June 1996); and Tena, *Derecho constitucional mexicano.*

[26] Tena, ibid.

[27] Reforming the Constitution to reinstate the Senate's power to approve expenditures has been suggested several times. In 1997, for example, Senator Rodríguez Lozano and Senator Lánz Cárdenas presented a bill designed to strengthen the legislative branch: they proposed "new rules for the approval of revenues and Senate intervention in the approval of expenditures and public accounts" (see *Iniciativa para el fortalecimiento del Poder Legislativo*, Proceedings of the Senate of the Republic, November 10, 1997).

[28] When constitutional reforms to create the *Auditoría Superior de la Federación* were passed in 1999, it was established that the ASF would take full effect and authority once its bylaw (*Ley Superior de Fiscalización*) was passed. The bylaw was submitted to the lower house, approved in December 1999, and sent to the Senate for approval. However, the Senate amended the bill and approved it in April 2000, thereby requiring submission to the lower house for its opinion, amendments (if any), and approval. As of August 2000, the bylaw had not yet received final approval.

[29] The Federal District Department, that is, the government of Mexico City, had been a unit subject to the auditing power of the Chamber of Deputies and its *Contaduría Mayor de Hacienda.* As part of a reform enacted in 1994 and effective in 1995, the finances, operations, and the Public Account of the Federal District Department are reviewed by the local Assembly of the Federal District through its own *Contaduría Mayor* (see *Estatuto de gobierno del Distrito Federal*, published in the *Diario Oficial de la Federación*, July 26, 1994).

[30] A whole set of laws, bylaws, and legal provisions regulate the functioning of the Mexican federal government. The most important are the following: Political Constitution of the United Mexican States; the annual *Ley de Ingresos* (Revenue Bill) and *Presupuesto de Egresos* (Budget Bill); *Ley de Presupuesto, Contabilidad y Gasto Público* (Law of Budget, Accounting, and Public Spending); *Ley Federal de Responsabilidades de los Servidores Públicos* (Federal Law of Civil Servants' Responsibilities); *Ley General de Deuda Pública* (General Law of Public Debt); *Ley Orgánica de la Administración Pública Federal* (Federal Law of the Federal Public Administration); *Ley Federal de Entidades*

Paraestateles (Federal Law of Semi-State Entities); *Ley de Planeación* (Planning Law); *Ley de Adquisiciones y Obras Públicas* (Law of Government Purchases and Public Works); *Ley General de Bienes Nacionales* (General Law of National Properties); and *Ley Orgánica de la Contaduría Mayor de Hacienda* (Federal Law of the Treasury Accounting Office) (see *Legislación de la Administración Pública Federal, 1995* [Mexico City: Ediciones Delma, 1995]).

[31] For a description of the internal organization and resources of the U.S. counterpart, see Harry S. Havens, *The Evolution of the General Accounting Office: From Voucher Audits to Program Evaluations* (Washington, D.C.: U.S. General Accounting Office, 1990). For a description in Spanish of the GAO's functions and structure, see Leobardo J. Mendoza, "La Fiscalización de la administración pública en México" (M.A. thesis, Facultad Latinoamericana de Ciencias Sociales, 1996), pp. 65–69.

[32] See Articles 2, 5, and 6 of *Ley Orgánica de la Contaduría Mayor de Hacienda,* 1978. The previous Federal Law (1936) did not mention the appointment, duration of term, or removal of the *contador mayor.* See also Neri Alvaro Cepeda, "La Contaduría Mayor de Hacienda: Legislación y análisis" (B.A. thesis, Universidad Autónoma de Guadalajara, 1974), pp. 26–41.

[33] When the PRI group in the Chamber supported Mr. Castillo Ayala as the best candidate for *contador mayor* in 1990, opposition parties argued that his past work in the government and his connections with officials in the administration would limit his neutrality and bias his performance. Congressman Pablo Gómez of the Democratic Revolutionary Party argued that there was even political loyalty between the nominee and Carlos Salinas (see *Diary of Debates,* November 27, 1990; *La Jornada,* November 30, 1990; and *El Universal,* December 4, 1990).

[34] *Diary of Debates,* September 2, 1977, and November 23, 1982.

[35] An interesting and contrasting case regarding this matter is the *Court de Comptes* in France, the auditing office that oversees the public sector. This agency enjoys the highest social and political prestige in that country. According to ministers and personnel from that organization, the *Court de Comptes* attracts the most qualified people, especially from the prestigious National School of Public Administration. That recruiting pattern is supported by a civil service system within the *Court,* which does not exist in the Mexican *Contaduría.* According to a French civil servant, "to become a minister within the *Court de Comptes* constitutes a lifetime achievement" (personal interviews conducted in Paris, France, July 22–24, 1996).

[36] The new bill approved by the House in December 1999 that created the *Auditoría Superior de la Federación* reduced the oversight time period by about five months.

[37]See Article 74 of the 1917 Mexican Constitution and Article 42 of *Ley de Presupuesto, Contabilidad y Gasto Público, 1994,* in *Legislación de la Administración Pública Federal.*

[38] Article 30 of the proposed *Ley de Fiscalización Superior de la Federación* (as detailed in note 28).

[39] See Article 31 of the *Contaduría's* Federal Law and Articles 108, 109, and 110 of the 1917 Mexican Constitution.

[40] This conclusion was derived from personal analysis and from several interviews with members of the Supervisory Committee and personnel from the *Contaduría,* including the *contador mayor* and the office's director of legal affairs.

[41] It can certainly be argued, however, that more effective action on the part of the *Contaduría* would have helped limit such corruption.

[42] Finding and constructing performance indicators was the most difficult research task encountered in the process of this study. The *Contaduría* lacks orderly and complete records of its activities. Usually, methodologies and formats change from year to year. In some cases, records are not available; in other cases, certain information is not available to the public. *Contaduría* officials usually consider information to be proprietary, and they perceive researchers as journalists looking for sensational news stories. Therefore, indicators used in this work can only gauge actual performance; their validity is constrained by the quality of available information.

[43] These numbers are based on the *Contaduría's* preliminary reports and final reports for 1975–88. Each report consists of several volumes totaling several hundred pages each. The task of constructing these figures took months to complete. For the years not covered, it was impossible to get information either because records were not available or because information was presented in different formats.

[44] Personal interview, August 10, 1995.

[45] Estimates are based on *Contaduría* reports for various years.

[46] For a discussion of the literature on information costs, see Paul Milgrom and John Roberts, *Economics, Organization and Management* (Englewood Cliffs, N.J.: Prentice-Hall, 1992); Thráinn Eggertsson, *Economic Behavior and Institutions* (Cambridge and New York: Cambridge University Press, 1990), chap. 1; and Douglass C. North, *Institutions, Institutional Change, and Economic Performance* (Cambridge and New York: Cambridge University Press, 1990), chap. 4.

[47] The proposed *Ley de Fiscalización Superior de la Federación,* which is expected to be approved by Congress in late 2000 (see note 28) proposes an

Oversight Committee (*Comisión de Vigilancia*) to oversee the ASF. This committee would have the power to create an Evaluation and Control Unit (*Unidad de Evaluación y Control*) and would be able to hire outside consultants to achieve this end. Therefore, this committee would have more authority and resources to monitor the monitoring agency, despite losing its constitutional status.

[48] Personal interview, April 5, 1995.

[49] Personal interview, August 16, 1995.

[50] The scientific validity of the number of references during floor debates as an indicator of the relative importance and performance of the Supervisory Committee is questionable. But it is one of the very few "objective" indicators that could be found.

[51] The question of how to monitor a monitor is an important one in the new institutionalist approach. In particular, the principal-agent theory has dealt with the issue of how a principal oversees an agent in order to verify adequate performance. For a review of these topics, see Eggertsson, *Economic Behavior and Institutions*, chap. 6; Harold Demsetz, "The Theory of the Firm Revisited," in *The Nature of the Firm: Origins, Evolution and Development*, ed. Oliver E. Williamson and Sidney O. Winter (Oxford and New York: Oxford University Press, 1991); Armen Alchian and Harold Demsetz, "Production, Information Costs, and Economic Organization," *American Economic Review* 62 (1972): 777–95; and Joseph E. Stiglitz, "Principal and Agent," in *The New Palgrave*, ed. John Eatwell (New York: Norton, 1989). For an application of the principal-agent theory to the U.S. Congress, see Barry R. Weingast, "The Congressional-Bureaucratic System: A Principal-Agent Perspective (with Applications to the SEC)," *Public Choice* 44 (1984): 147–91.

CHAPTER THREE

INVESTIGATIVE COMMITTEES

CONGRESS HAS OTHER RELEVANT VEHICLES TO USE TO MONITOR THE government's operations in Mexico: the *comisiones de investigación* (investigative committees), which are formed in response to deputies' special petitions to the Chamber seeking to analyze and investigate the operations of public enterprises. These cases of legislative oversight have received scant attention in the academic literature and, until a few years ago, very little press coverage as well. Nevertheless, these committees constitute a very powerful means of exercising legislative control over the executive branch of the Mexican government.

CONSTITUTIONAL FOUNDATION: ARTICLE 93

Investigative committees have their foundation in the third paragraph of Article 93 of the 1917 Mexican Constitution, which states:

> The Chambers, at the request of one-fourth of their members in the case of Deputies, and one-half in the case of Senators, have the power to form committees to investigate the operations of ... decentralized federal agencies and enterprises in which the State has majority participation. The results of the investigations shall be made known to the Federal Executive.[1]

This third paragraph was added to Article 93 only in 1977, as part of a major political reform promoted by then president José López Portillo and his minister of the interior, Jesús Reyes Heroles. The reform was aimed at stimulating an increase in the representation of minority parties and emergent political forces.[2] As part of the effort to stimulate the "voice of the minorities," the reform gave extraordinary oversight authority to congressional minorities: one-fourth of the deputies would have the power to form committees to investigate the operations of public enterprises and decentralized government agencies. With that threshold of 25 percent, the opposition has had the numbers to request the creation of committees since 1979, the year in which opposition deputies came to account for exactly one-fourth of the Chamber's total membership.[3] Opposition membership has surpassed that percentage in all subsequent legislatures.[4] In 1997, opposition parties—with 52 percent of the seats—represented an absolute majority en bloc; and in the 58th Legislature (2000–2003), which took office on September 1, 2000, opposition parties account for an even larger share of seats—58 percent. In the 58th Legislature, the Institutional Revolutionary Party will be part of the opposition (along with the Democratic Revolutionary Party and other minor parties) for the first time in its history.

Since the adoption of the 1917 Mexican Constitution, the first paragraph of Article 93 has required cabinet ministers to report to Congress "on the state of their respective branches" on a yearly basis.[5] A second paragraph was added to the same article in 1974, and this change empowered Congress to summon cabinet ministers and heads of administrative departments, as well as directors of decentralized agencies and public enterprises, whenever their reports and information were deemed necessary or useful for lawmaking or congressional analysis.[6] However, these powers to summon ministers and agency heads and request information from them were limited in and of themselves, because legislators could not pursue investigations beyond questions and answers that arose in Congress. This limitation became increasingly evident as the Mexican Public Administration grew in size and complexity, and hearings alone became a very restricted way of obtaining information.

During the 1970s, for example, the public enterprise sector grew rapidly. Consequently, a broadened set of instruments became necessary to control mismanagement and corruption. For instance, in

Table 3.1
Growth of the Public Enterprise Sector, 1970–94

Year	Number of Enterprises
1970	179
1972	333
1975	504
1977	899
1980	903
1982	1,155
1985	941
1988	412
1994	216

Sources: For 1970–74: Carlos Pérez, *Empresas públicas. Aspectos económicos* (Mexico City: CIDE, 1976); for 1975: *Cuenta de la Hacienda Pública Federal;* for 1977–81: *Manual de Organización de la APF* (Mexico City: Presidencia de la República, 1982); for 1982–94: *El proceso de enajenación de entidades paraestatales* (Mexico City: Secretaría de Hacienda, 1994).

1970 there were only 179 public enterprises; at the time of the 1977 reform their number had grown to 899, accounting for about one-half of the government's budget; and by 1982 there were 1,155. (The numbers for selected years are presented in table 3.1.) Since congressional hearings became powerless as a means of controlling this increasingly huge bureaucracy, Paragraph 3 of Article 93 was enacted in 1977. Paragraph 3 strengthened Congress's oversight authority over this large bureaucracy, because Congress acquired the power not only to summon functionaries but also to conduct audits, on-site investigations, and all necessary related investigations in order to obtain firsthand information about the operation of the public enterprise sector.

It is important to recall that the Mexican Public Administration is composed of two main areas: the *sector central* (or central government) and the so-called *sector paraestatal* (the semistate sector). As of 1994, the *sector central* consisted of 17 *Secretarías de Estado* (ministries) and the Office of the President. The *sector paraestatal* was

Figure 3.1
Domain of Oversight Authority

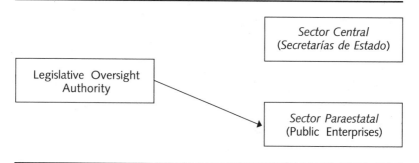

made up of public enterprises (enterprises with majority state participation) and decentralized government agencies. It is precisely this domain—the *sector paraestatal*—that is subject to legislative investigation according to Article 93, Paragraph 3.[7] (See figure 3.1.)

Many have suggested, however, that investigations should include the central government as well, not only because of its political and budgetary importance (as in the case of the Public Education Ministry), but also because the downsizing and privatization of public enterprises and decentralized government agencies during the 1980s and 1990s have decreased the relative significance of the *sector paraestatal* in economic and financial terms. Just as the exponential growth of the semistate sector in the 1970s made oversight a necessity, the reduction in its size to little more than 200 entities has decreased its relevance. According to Mora-Donatto "nowadays it is evident that the main subject for investigative committees is all but obsolete due to the 'privatization wave' that ... reduced the administration to a minimum." Consequently, this author recommended "expanding the domain of investigative committees ... to include any subject that concerns the public interest."[8] Although it might be an exaggeration to assert that the *sector paraestatal* is obsolete, it is certainly true that its relative importance as part of the federal budget has diminished considerably since the end of the 1980s. Therefore, legislative oversight would be strengthened if investigative committees were able to review the whole executive branch of the government, the *sector central* included.[9]

Since its enactment in 1977, the third paragraph of Article 93 has been a source of controversy because of its ambiguous phrasing: "The Chambers, at the request of one-fourth of their members in the case of Deputies ... have the power to form committees to investigate...." This wording does not clarify the extent or the meaning of the phrase "power to form committees." On the one hand, one can argue that a minority (at least one-fourth of the Chamber) has the right to *form* investigative committees, either with or without the support of the rest of the Chamber (the majority). On the other hand, one can argue that a minority may have the right to *request* the formation of such committees, but that final approval must come from the majority of the Chamber, in accordance with the majority principle that guides parliamentary procedures in Mexico.

In 1977, when approval of this paragraph was being discussed, an opposition legislator suggested that the article should say, instead: "by a *resolution* of a minority, investigative committees must be formed" (italics added), a phrase that does not allow for the interpretation of "the minority requesting, but the majority deciding." According to this legislator, the original phrasing was ambiguous and left to the PRI majority the right to decide whether or not to form investigative committees. "It is not a matter of minorities requesting, but of minorities having the authority to decide on the formation of these oversight bodies. If that ambiguous wording is not changed, the majority will retain the right to approve or not approve formation of such committees in accordance with their political interests."[10] The Chamber rejected this proposal, and since then the original wording has left much of the actual implementation of the article to the legal (and political) interpretation given by different legislators from various parties.

HISTORY OF INVESTIGATIVE COMMITTEES

Since its enactment in December 1977, Paragraph 3 of Article 93 has been implemented on only a few occasions. Whenever requests to apply it have been made, legal and technical controversies have delayed its implementation. Indeed, during the last 23 years, only seven investigative committees have actually been formed; committees were requested in five other cases but rejected by the PRI majority, who cited legal considerations. This dearth of cases is especially shameful, given the large number instances of corruption and mismanagement within public enterprises that have come to light in the last decades.

Telephone Tapping Within TELMEX

In early November 1979, almost two years after passage of the third paragraph of Article 93, a group of 103 deputies (25.75 percent of the Chamber)—most from opposition parties but including a few members of the PRI—requested that a committee be formed to investigate accusations that the telephones of union leaders, nongovernmental organizations, opposition party members, and the media had been tapped.[11] The request asked for an investigation into possible espionage practices within TELMEX (*Teléfonos de México*), a state-owned telephone monopoly at the time. The request was analyzed by the *Gran Comisión,* which finally supported the formation of the committee and proposed members for inclusion.[12] The request was accepted, and the TELMEX Investigative Committee was approved and created on November 21, 1979.

The new committee consisted of seven deputies—four from the PRI and three from the opposition—and was presided over by a PRI member.[13] In contrast to what would have been expected from this investigative body—taking into account that it was the first use of its new legislative power—the committee met just a few times and did very little. Its work was basically confined to requesting reports and information from TELMEX and from the Ministry of the Interior and to holding one meeting with high-level TELMEX officials. After four months of existence, on March 25, 1980, the TELMEX Investigative Committee issued a final report, which contained three main conclusions:

1. There are an infinite number of ways to interfere with telephone communications, and that makes it technically possible to illegally interfere with telephone lines [*sic*].

2. Laws regulating telecommunications are deficient and do not cover the case of telephone tapping. Therefore, it is imperative to legislate this matter and make espionage illegal in order to prevent its proliferation.

3. The Chamber's Justice Committee is entrusted with the task of proposing a bill to prohibit telephone tapping and presenting it during the next period of sessions.[14]

According to Pablo Gómez (Mexican Communist Party), a member of the committee and the principal advocate for the investigation, the TELMEX Committee spent its time protecting government officials instead of getting to the heart of the problem: in his words, *"los diputados investigadores del espionaje no investigaron."*[15] For Gómez, who did not sign the committee's final report, legal and political factors explained the obstacles faced by the TELMEX Investigative Committee:

On the juridical side, House committees lack legal powers to summon government officials to interrogate them. Officials can appear before a committee on a voluntary basis [*sic*].[16] On the political side, the TELMEX Committee had a PRI majority [four out of seven members], who tried, from the very first, to avoid any legal responsibility for linking government officials to espionage activities.[17]

During the four months of its operation, the TELMEX Committee maintained a low profile within the Chamber; it received very little press coverage; and, most important, it did not expose anything that was not known prior to its creation.[18] The final report's conclusion that telephone tapping is "technically possible" certainly did not require a legislative committee's time and effort; and its only recommendation was that the matter "be legislated." The committee never mentioned who was responsible for the reported espionage, nor did it find or disclose any specific technical means by which telephones in Mexico were tapped. As a result, the committee never proposed any sanctions. It is fair to say that the committee's recommendations had no impact at all: telephone tapping continued to be a common practice in Mexico, and only in 1995 did the Chamber legislate this matter, and then only in response to an executive branch initiative.[19]

Laguna Verde's Nuclear Threat

Laguna Verde, a state-owned nuclear power plant in the State of Veracruz, is administered by the Federal Electricity Commission (CFE). *Laguna Verde* began operation in October 1988, but in the months preceding its opening, university students, journalists, opposition party members, and members of nongovernmental organizations protested the initiation of operations at the plant, primarily out of security concerns, some of which were not necessarily well founded. (The 1986 accident at the Chernobyl nuclear power plant was still on people's minds.)

The opposition of specific groups to *Laguna Verde* was evident in Congress in early October 1988. Members of every opposition party, except the Socialist Popular Party, demanded either the cancellation of the project or the postponement of its opening, unless further security investigations were conducted and certifications made. Congressman Ciro Mayén (National Democratic Front) suggested the creation of an investigative committee—based on Article 93—to study the security conditions at *Laguna Verde* before the nuclear reactor was charged up and operations were initiated.[20] His request was supported and signed by 136 of the 500 members of the Chamber (27.2 percent), yet the committee was not formed, as it should have been according to the Constitution. The request was made again a week later by two other opposition members—Congressmen Jesús Ortega (Mexican Socialist Party) and Ismael Yañez (Democratic Center)—who called for the immediate formation of an investigative committee and postponement of *Laguna Verde*'s operation unless the Chamber issued an opinion.[21] Again, instead of a committee being formed automatically, the request was sent to the *Comisión de Gobernación* for analysis and evaluation; the reason given was the controversy over whether a petition from the minority was sufficient for the formation of an investigative committee or whether the majority's approval was also necessary. From that date forward, the request was never brought to the floor again, nor was an investigative committee ever formed, despite extensive press coverage.

In the midst of this debate, however, a majority of PRI members in both the Chamber and the Senate voted in favor of a statement that publicly manifested their political support for the *Laguna Verde* operation. This vote of confidence took the opposition by surprise, which, as expected, voted against the measure and pushed its demand to suspend the project. In the end, *Laguna Verde* began operations in late 1988, and the investigative committee was never formed. Fortunately, no accident has ever been reported at the nuclear power plant.[22]

Illegal Contracting Within PEMEX Oil Company

In 1986, Congressman Jorge Alcocer, a member of the United Socialist Party, accused the chief executive officer of the PEMEX Oil Company, Mario Beteta, and a business associate of entering into an illegal contract with two oil tankers. The allegation received no legislative support and was therefore dismissed. Two years later, however, in a legislature with a stronger opposition presence, a few deputies and members of the Oil Workers Union (a PRI organization) revisited the issue and again accused Beteta and Isidoro Rodríguez (a transportation entrepreneur) of collusion in entering into an illegal and expensive contract in 1985 "against the interests of the enterprise and the people of Mexico." According to the deputies, the contract cost PEMEX millions of dollars and violated its internal rules and standard operating procedures. These denunciations provoked a political scandal in October 1988, which involved PEMEX officials, private entrepreneurs, and even the president of the republic, all of whom were accused of having participated in, covered up, or at least permitted the illegal contract.

At the request of the opposition, on October 20, 1988, the House approved the creation of a special committee—composed of members of all parties—to follow up on the accusation and to ensure that the attorney general investigated the case. Because this special committee was not based on Article 93, its constitutional and legal authority was limited. In fact, the committee was in existence for only one month; and on November 18, the PRI majority approved the committee's report, which cleared the PEMEX chief and top officials of any burden or legal responsibility associated with the disputed contracts. The adjournment of the special committee and the exoneration of the accused created a political scandal that was widely covered in the media.

A week after the creation of the special committee, Gerardo Medina (Democratic Revolutionary Party)—with the support of 127 deputies (25.4 percent)—requested that an investigative committee be formed, based on Article 93, to analyze and to review PEMEX's contracting procedures. The request was sent on to the *Comisión de Gobernación* for an opinion but was never brought to the floor. It is surprising that opposition parties never insisted on using Article 93 to support the PEMEX investigation, relying instead on a special committee whose jurisdiction and authority were based only on the Congressional Federal Law, which has narrower powers and lower status than the Constitution. This case reveals that opposition deputies may not have even known the extent and authority of the powers conferred upon them by Article 93 and, therefore, were unable to build a more solid case.

Liquidation of the National Bank of Fishing and Ports

On December 28, 1989, the executive branch sent a bill to Congress seeking to abrogate the federal law that supported the existence and operations of BANPESCA, the state-owned National Bank of Fishing and Ports. The reasons the authorities gave for the dissolution of this development bank were that it was in financial bankruptcy, that it had an overburdened debt and a huge portfolio *vencido,* and that other government agencies could achieve its objectives and perform its functions better. As soon as the bill was presented on the floor of the Chamber, a heated debate was initiated by many opposition Congress members, who suspected that the real causes of the bankruptcy were the illegal granting of credits and loans, corruption, and mismanagement—all of which, they believed, characterized the way the bank operated. Fishermen's associations rapidly joined the debate, accusing bank officials of being responsible for the financial disaster and of misappropriating funds and loans.[23] Congressman Jesús Rojo (PAN) rejected the bill to abrogate BANPESCA's Federal Law and, on that same day, proposed the formation of an investigative committee, based on Article 93, to review the operations of the bank and the reasons for its bankruptcy. Supported by 175 deputies (35 percent of the Chamber), the request claimed that, before the Chamber could vote on the bill, the legislature had to inquire and get firsthand information about the real causes behind the bank's failure.

As soon as the request was made, the customary legal controversy over the meaning of Article 93 erupted, with opposition deputies insisting that the minority's request was sufficient for the automatic formation of the committee, and PRI legislators arguing that the minority's request was simply a necessary step for the creation of the investigative body and was subject to the majority's approval. Trinidad Lanz (PRI) maintained that Congress was a multiparty body "whose decisions are made by majority principle, and it would be antidemocratic if minorities could decide upon the wishes of the majority." After many hours of interparty debate and intraparty negotiations—in which the coalition and unity among opposition parties contrasted with the division among *priístas* (PRI members) over whether or not to support the opposition's demand—the BANPESCA Investigative Committee was finally created. Nevertheless, the PRI's interpretation of Article 93 prevailed: the minority had the right to request the committee, but the majority had the power to actually create it. As a consequence, the opposition had to submit its request to the floor for approval (counter to its original argument that such a decision did not have to go through that voting procedure) and the PRI voted in favor; indeed, the creation of the committee was approved unanimously,

In the weeks following the committee's creation, the opposition criticized deficiencies in its work: various deputies claimed that the committee had met only four times, and, most important, that the information it had requested and received from the government was inadequate, insufficient, and filtered in order to cover up past irregularities and illegal practices. One of the main obstacles the committee faced was that much of the information requested was never disclosed by the authorities, who cited the *Secreto Bancario*—a law that protects investors and financial institutions from disclosing information about their clients' transactions and investments. Consequently, the committee was unable to properly analyze the granting of loans and credits or evaluate the internal financial operations of the bank.[24]

The opposition requested an extension of the 60-day period originally established for the committee's work, but on April 24, 1990, the PRI members of the committee presented a final report to the floor, about which the opposition deputies had been informed only the night before it was to be presented.[25] The main points in the final report were the following:

1. The committee had received and analyzed sufficient information; however, some information had not been disclosed because of *Secreto Bancario* considerations.

2. On April 20, committee members had met with BANPESCA officials, who responded to questions posed by committee members.

3. The fact that this committee lacked sufficient authority to broaden the examination of this case did not mean that the investigation was over. There were other instances that needed to be examined and executive authorities who could continue this task, correct the irregularities detected, if any, and eventually sanction those found responsible.

4. The results did not mean that the committee's findings lacked relevance; on the contrary, the final report was extensive and responsive to the objectives that the investigative committee had established.[26]

This final report provoked another heated debate, because the conclusions did not include the opposition's points of view and did not mention the restrictions that the committee had faced. The opposition wanted to extend the period of investigation, but the PRI majority rejected this initiative. Under these circumstances, the legislative branch (with a PRI majority) decided to send the conclusions of the investigation to the executive branch, in accordance with the text of Article 93, which states that "the Federal Executive shall be informed of the results of the investigations."

After exhausting the Chamber's investigative options, PAN members decided to lodge a criminal complaint before the *Ministerio Público* (a unit within the Office of the Attorney General and thus dependent on the executive branch; it is comparable to the U.S. attorney's office) against those found responsible for BANPESCA's bankruptcy. Authentic Mexican Revolutionary Party members filed a similar complaint, and the Ministry of the Treasury lodged an accusation as well. As a result of these complaints, in the following months, the attorney general conducted a thorough investigation and arrested a former director general (Pedro Galicia Estrada) and several mid-level bank officials. Three months after the committee adjourned, 13 individuals had been arrested and 264 criminal and civil trials were in progress, but mainly as a result of the attorney general's efforts.[27] At the time, several opposition deputies complained that the committee had not gone to the heart of the problem and that those who had been arrested were merely mid-level officials, not the "big shots" behind the corruption and misappropriation of funds.[28] Yet, for other deputies, "these actions invalidated the accusations that the investigative committee had not served any purpose other than to protect BANPESCA officials."[29]

The assessment of the results of the BANPESCA Investigative Committee is a controversial matter. On the one hand, the committee converted the BANPESCA liquidation into a political scandal that attracted wide media coverage. Had the Chamber not denounced irregularities and had the committee not been formed, the BANPESCA issue might have been an administrative procedure that received no public attention at all. Even though the BANPESCA Committee faced restrictions in its actual operation, the resulting publicity and media exposure may have been instrumental in forcing the executive branch (including the president of the republic) to initiate subsequent investigations from within the administration (that is, the Office of the Attorney General) and to arrest and prosecute several BANPESCA officials. As a result, the individuals involved were incarcerated and some missing funds were repaid.[30]

The opposition's success in bringing the BANPESCA scandal to the national forefront was facilitated, first, by the group's strength within the 54th Legislature (1988–91)—about 48 percent. Second, the opposition was able to take advantage of the relative weakness of President Salinas's new administration, which, even one year after its inauguration, continued to be tarnished by accusations that it had been fraudulently elected in 1988. In such an environment, the executive branch was forced to negotiate in order to establish and enlarge its governing coalition; the formation of the BANPESCA Committee might have been one of the strategies used to avoid any further political conflict that would have caused its public image to deteriorate. The government's "permissiveness" in allowing the creation of the BANPESCA Investigative Committee must be understood in this context.[31]

Some shortcomings are evident in the way the BANPESCA Investigative Committee's work was conducted, however. First, the procedures to create the committee were controversial as a result of the opposition's acceptance, in practice, of the PRI majority's interpretation of Article 93 (that the minority may request, but the majority must approve). That precedent was harmful for subsequent cases in which similar committees needed to be formed. Second, the committee did not use its legal and constitutional powers to require authorities to cooperate with the investigation: top-level officials were not summoned before the committee, and financial authorities were able to provide information at their discretion. Finally, the committee abdicated its investigative responsibilities and concluded its task by asking the attorney general and other executive branch officials to continue the investigation that the committee's deputies were supposed to conduct. For these reasons, the committee did not produce any concrete results and, therefore, could not initiate the prosecution of anyone based on its own investigations.

Electricity Rates Charged
by the Federal Electricity Commission

On March 14, 1990, Pedro Acosta Palomino (a PAN deputy) re-quested the formation of an investigative committee, based on Ar-ticle 93, "to conduct a thorough review of the accounting and financial operations of the *Comisión Federal de Electricidad* (Fed-eral Electricity Commission) in order to determine the causes for the drastic increase in electricity rates."[32] In the previous weeks, the CFE, a state-owned monopoly that generates and distributes electrical power in Mexico, had increased its rates and fees, and in response to that move, opposition deputies presented the request, which was supported by 135 deputies (27 percent of the Chamber).[33] The re-quest was not automatically translated into the creation of an actual committee but was sent to the Energy Committee for an opinion. However, the Energy Committee neither made a report nor issued any opinion on the request, which got lost among other legislative activities and issues.

Once again, on December 21, 1990, nine months after the original request had been made, the request was presented to the floor. This time there were new matters for the proposed investigative commit-tee to look into because, in May 1990, the CFE had initiated a new charge, called "Charge 11–48," the purpose of which—according to authorities—was to collect money for the construction of new power plants, maintenance of existing ones, and improvement of the company's services. Even though consumers and political groups nationwide had opposed the new charge, the request was ignored again and failed to receive sufficient attention from the media or from opposition deputies themselves.

In the first months of 1991, opposition members in the Chamber began to persistently criticize the CFE's new pricing policy, claiming that it harmed the economic well-being of households and stating that the increase in electricity rates would not have been necessary if the CFE had been managed more efficiently and honestly. The oppo-sition declared that Charge 11–48 was illegal, and for the third time, on April 29, 1991, an investigative committee was requested before the floor—13 months after the original request had been presented. This time the request received sufficient attention from the Chamber, and predictably, the customary and controversial debate over the extent and the meaning of Article 93 ensued. As usual, the PRI stated that it would be antidemocratic for minorities to make decisions about the wishes of the majority and argued that, while minorities had the right to petition, the formation of investigative committees was a decision to be made by the entire Chamber. The opposition argued that, if that were the correct interpretation of the law, then it would be "unnecessary to have an article in which it is established that 25 percent of deputies are required to request and form a committee," since, according to the Congressional Federal Law, even one deputy has the right to present a petition before the floor.[34] "If minorities could only request, but not decide upon, the creation of committees, then the third paragraph of Article 93 of the Constitution would be unnecessary and meaningless."[35]

The PRI intended to reject the request by submitting it to a floor vote two weeks later, but the opposition left the assembly room just moments before the vote in order to prevent what they perceived to be an unconstitutional act from taking place. Therefore, a committee to investigate the CFE was never formed, but the opposition was able to avoid setting a harmful and illegal precedent: submitting the request for the creation of an investigative committee to a floor vote, even though—according to the opposition—the committee should have been created automatically because the request was made by the required minority of 25 percent.[36] Just after the opposition request had been dismissed, the PRI parliamentary group proposed that the *Contaduría Mayor de Hacienda* (Congress's Treasury Accounting Office, which reports to the legislative branch through its Supervisory Committee) audit the CFE for the purpose of assessing its financial situation. This proposal was immediately submitted to the floor and approved by the majority. The results of the audit exposed an enterprise that was overburdened by debts and facing a critical financial situation. Nevertheless, no one was held responsible or prosecuted for mismanaging the monopoly.[37]

Mismanagement of INFONAVIT

On February 19, 1992, Congressman Juan de Dios Castro (PAN), with the support of 128 deputies (25.6 percent), requested the creation of an investigative committee to conduct a review of the finances and operations of INFONAVIT, a government agency responsible for constructing subsidized housing for workers and for providing credits and loans for acquisition of the properties. INFONAVIT had frequently been accused of corruption, mismanagement, inefficiency, and an overburdened bureaucracy that made its administrative operation too onerous. In the early months of 1992, a new federal law regulating INFONAVIT was about to be discussed in Congress and legislative attention was naturally focused on the functioning of the agency; therefore, it was a propitious time for the opposition to benefit from exposing possible corruption within the housing agency.

Because the full Chamber was not in session in February of that year, PRI members of the *Comisión Permanente* argued that the petition had to be presented before the full Chamber once it was in regular session again and, therefore, rejected even the possibility of discussing the request. Once the House was in full session, the PAN parliamentary group presented the request to the floor again on April 30, 1992. The usual constitutional and legal controversies surrounding the interpretation of Article 93 arose, with the opposition once again claiming that the request did not need to go through the traditional legislative process. After a long debate, the PRI, going even further than it had previously, rejected even the possibility of discussing the request in the Chamber. The treatment given to this solicitation invalidated, in practice, the extent and meaning of minority deputies' rights, which were expressly granted in Article 93.

It is important to recall that, at other times (such as in the *Laguna Verde* and PEMEX cases), investigative committees had not been formed—not as a result of an open vote in the Chamber, but rather as a consequence of requests being intentionally lost among other legislative issues. Nevertheless, at least the solicitations had been formally submitted to the House and sent on to existing congressional committees. In other words, although it was anomalous that those requests were not translated into the creation of investigative committees, it happened because PRI members surreptitiously blocked the process, not because of a formal and visible violation of the law of the land. In contrast, when it was faced with the request for an INFONAVIT committee, the Chamber publicly and formally submitted the request as part of a legislative process that was inappropriate for the solicitation at hand, openly violating the Constitution and establishing a damaging precedent for future applications of Article 93.

Corruption in CONASUPO, I

In February 1995, three months after former president Carlos Salinas de Gortari had left office, the new attorney general arrested Salinas's brother, Raúl Salinas, as the prime suspect in ordering the assassination of José F. Ruiz Massieu, a former secretary general of the PRI and a national political figure.[38] In the course of the investigation, some evidence was found not only showing Raúl Salinas's involvement in the plot but also tying him to corruption cases. Since murder was the original reason for launching the investigation, in the months following his arrest, the corruption and tax evasion charges became the basis for parallel investigations. One of the most notorious corruption cases associated with the name of Raúl Salinas was that of CONASUPO, a huge state-owned commercial food enterprise, where he had been planning director and a high-level official during the late 1980s and early 1990s.

The political scandal created by the arrest of Raúl Salinas, as well as the general climate of anger, animosity, and hostility toward the figure of former President Carlos Salinas—whom the general population was accusing of being responsible for the 1995 economic crisis and even of being the intellectual author of the assassination of 1994 PRI presidential candidate Luis Donaldo Colosio—created an environment in which the legislative branch was able to intervene in the investigation of corruption charges against Raúl Salinas. Specifically, on November 28, 1995, Independent Congressman Adolfo Aguilar Zínser requested the formation of an investigative committee to examine and review the operations of CONASUPO between

1982 and 1992, the years during which Raúl Salinas had worked there. The request was made with the support of 143 legislators (28.6 percent), most from the opposition but including a few from the PRI.[39]

This time there was no business-as-usual debate over the meaning of Article 93. In fact, PRI deputies did not even argue against the minority's right to petition for the formation of an investigative committee. Indeed, the solicitation was automatically sent to the *Comisión de Régimen y Concertación Política*,[40] not for the committee to render an opinion, but rather for it to propose members to serve on the investigative committee. Thus, the CONASUPO Investigative Committee was created as soon as the request was presented to the floor. The committee was composed of 16 members (9 from the PRI and 7 from the opposition) and presided over by a PRI deputy.[41] Over the next 10 months, the CONASUPO Committee worked intensely and received extensive media coverage. Its first step was to establish the scope of the investigation. In January 1996, eight investigative objectives were agreed upon, the most important of which were the following:

1. To analyze and review past audits of CONASUPO as well as its financial and accounting records;

2. To review the importation of powdered milk from Ireland between 1986 and 1988, which, according to the ecology group Greenpeace, had been contaminated by radioactive material;

3. To review the importation and possible overpricing of contaminated grain from China and the United States; and

4. To review the 1992 privatization of MICONSA, a subsidiary plant of CONASUPO.

To carry out this large and complex investigative task, the committee hired two accounting firms to conduct the audits and to assist in its work. However, in the following weeks, opposition deputies on the committee began accusing—not always supported by the evidence—various former and current government ministers and officials of having caused some of the irregularities within CONASUPO, because some of the individuals had been closely related to its operations during the period that was under investigation.[42] Even President Ernesto Zedillo was mentioned as having illegally authorized CONASUPO's officials to make a subsidy payment to MASECA, a private tortilla emporium whose chief executive officer had been accused of being a partner of Raúl Salinas.[43] The unofficial accusations began to generate conflict among committee members, and as a consequence, PRI deputies started to restrict the flow of information given to opposition deputies. Indeed, PRI members and government officials accused the opposition of acting irresponsibly and of using confidential information for partisan and publicity purposes. For example, Jaime Serra, former minister of commerce (1988–94) and, as such, chair of CONASUPO's board of directors, threatened to sue those deputies who, without any legal evidence, had accused him of protecting Raúl Salinas as well as covering up Salinas's alleged corruption.[44]

During its existence, the investigative committee requested information from, and conducted meetings with, the director and high-level officials of CONASUPO, the minister of the comptrollership, and the attorney general. From the beginning, it was clear that this investigative committee—even with the assistance of two accounting firms—was unable, unqualified, and powerless to handle, classify, and analyze the volume of information coming from the archives of CONASUPO and other relevant government sources.[45] As with other legislative committees, most of the members of the CONASUPO Committee had no previous oversight experience or financial background. Even worse, most of them had never even been deputies before—an obvious limitation when dealing with such a politically important and visible issue. As expected, opposition deputies charged that authorities were not disclosing certain information and that some mid-level CONASUPO officials—who had relevant and firsthand information about Raúl Salinas's operations—were being coerced, extorted, and bribed to prevent them from talking.[46] The deputies also accused the PRI majority on the committee (9 out of 16) of restricting the scope of the investigation and of trying to block further investigations.

By late August, the two accounting firms had finished their audits and financial reviews of CONASUPO and delivered them to the committee. In early September, opposition deputies were alerted to the PRI's plans to give a *carpetazo* to the CONASUPO investigation, that is, notice of their intention to close the case as rapidly as possible in order to avoid further examination and implication of more people.[47] As anticipated, the PRI members on the committee completed the final report of the investigation and presented it to the floor on September 26, 1996, with the following main conclusions:

1. The committee requested that executive branch authorities continue the investigations of two of CONASUPO's subsidiaries, DICONSA and MICONSA.

2. The committee also requested that executive branch authorities continue to investigate the accusation that CONASUPO had imported contaminated grain from China and the United States.

3. The payments made by CONASUPO to MASECA in 1988 were found to be totally legal and to have been carried out in accordance with internal rules and procedures.[48]

4. The levels of radioactive contamination of the powdered milk imported from Ireland were so low that consumers' health had not been put at risk.

5. There was no evidence that imported milk and grain had been overpriced.

6. In the case of the importation of Chinese beans, serious irregularities had affected the finances of the enterprise. (The committee mentioned two mid-level CONASUPO officials as the individuals responsible for these actions and requested further investigation and legal action against them.)

7. The committee requested that officials in the executive branch continue the investigation of the privatization of a branch of CONASUPO in Atlacomulco, in the State of Mexico.

Obviously, the report generated anger and criticism from the opposition, for whom the document did not present the whole story, did not mention the obstructions and limitations the committee had faced, and did not delve into the heart of the problem. Opposition members accused the PRI of having produced the report without their participation, thus protecting and covering up for government officials. The opposition demanded a meeting with representatives of the two accounting firms to find out their precise perceptions and opinions about the conclusions and requested an extension of the investigation period.[49] In the midst of this adverse environment, on October 8, 1996, the PRI majority voted to dissolve the CONASUPO Committee, after which they declared that the legislative investigations had been completed. According to the PRI parliamentary group, future investigations would be, and should be, carried out by the attorney general and the minister of the comptrollership, both officials within the executive branch.[50] Thus, the committee officially disappeared after only 10 months of existence.

Congressman Adolfo Aguilar Zínser accused President Ernesto Zedillo of being responsible for shutting down the committee. According to the congressman, the accusation that the president was involved in an allegedly illegal payment made by CONASUPO in 1988, when he was minister of planning and budget, was the primary reason for the government's obstruction and ultimate termination of the committee's mandate. Aguilar believed that PRI members of the committee had never acted independently: the minister of the interior was supposedly in charge of monitoring and designing the strategy to be followed by the committee, whose chair, Deputy Manuel Hinojosa, had always been a political follower and subordinate of his (Hinojosa had worked for the interior minister when the latter was governor of the State of Mexico a few years earlier).[51]

Corruption in CONASUPO, II

On October 9, 1996, in repudiation of and disagreement with the unilateral decision to close down the CONASUPO Investigative Committee, Deputy Víctor Quintana (PRD) initiated a fast within the assembly room of the Chamber. A week later, after 58,000 signatures had been collected to demand that the case be reopened, Quintana concluded his fast. In a speech explaining his actions, Quintana demanded that CONASUPO be investigated by the *Comisión de Abasto, Distribución y Manejo de Bienes de Consumo*

(Committee on the Supply, Distribution, and Handling of Consumer Goods). As a result of pressure from opposition deputies and the media, the CONASUPO investigation was reopened in May 1997, but not through the same investigative body. This time, the PRI majority authorized the *Comisión de Abasto, Distribución y Manejo de Bienes de Consumo*—presided over by a PRD member—to request information and to follow up the investigative steps already underway within the Office of the Attorney General.

The reopening of the case coincided, not accidentally, with the publication of a news story in the *Washington Post* on May 12, 1997, which accused Raúl Salinas of crimes via the CONASUPO Company. The report stated that the U.S. Department of Justice was investigating Raúl Salinas's use of CONASUPO for criminal enterprises, which included money laundering, drug profiteering, and channeling other illicit money through CONASUPO's bank accounts and contracts in the United States. A focus of the story was whether Raúl Salinas had used CONASUPO to hide cocaine shipments into the United States and to launder money for a drug-trafficking cartel.

Supposedly, with the Chamber's approval for members of the *Comisión de Abasto, Distribución y Manejo de Bienes de Consumo* to request information from the attorney general, the CONASUPO investigation would be able to delve more deeply this time. However, the case received little attention and political support in the weeks after it was reopened. It was not until the inauguration of the 57th Legislature in September 1997—a year in which, for the first time in history, the PRI did not hold an absolute majority—that the case truly received a second wave of attention and political support. As a result, on October 30, 1997, the Chamber unanimously approved the re-creation of the CONASUPO Investigative Committee, this time based on the powers established in Article 93 of the Constitution.[52] Before the floor vote took place, the PRI, as usual, argued that Article 93 was ambiguous and that specific regulations should be established to guide the functioning of investigative committees.[53] Nevertheless, the formation of the second CONASUPO Investigative Committee was approved.

Months passed without concrete results. The investigation of Raúl Salinas continued, but mainly as a result of the government's accusation that he had been involved in the murder of Ruiz Massieu. On August 25, 1998, 10 months after the CONASUPO case was reopened, the committee hired two outside accounting firms—*Daza y Asociados* and *Cerro Blanco*—to review (1) CONASUPO's financial operations during the 1980s, (2) the privatization of some LICONSA plants in 1991 (*Aguascalientes* and *Delicias*), (3) the importation of radioactive milk in 1986 and 1988, and (4) some supposedly irregular payments made to MASECA. In early February 1999, *Daza y Asociados* concluded that corruption and mismanagement had cost CONASUPO about $9 billion (in U.S. dollars).[54] The report also stated that several government officials—including the ministers of trade and health—were found to be responsible for importing contaminated milk in 1986. According to *Daza y Asociados*, irregular payments of about $1.6 million were made to MASECA, and the privatization of some LICONSA plants showed evidence of major irregularities. Those responsible for this mismanagement and corruption, according to the accounting firm, included several members of President Carlos Salinas's cabinet, among them Finance Secretary Pedro Aspe and Comptrollership Secretary María Elena Vázquez Nava.

Many members of the investigative committee—especially those from the PRI—received the report with suspicion. After internal discussions, the report was found to be inconsistent and replete with arguments and conclusions that were not supported by hard facts. As a result, the report was sent back to the accounting firms for a review of their findings and conclusions. Margarita Pérez Gavilán (PAN), chair of the committee, reported that the committee had requested more precision from *Daza y Asociados*, including specific names of those found responsible for mismanagement and corruption, as well as the exact amount of missing funds. It is important to recall that just two years earlier, in 1996, two other auditing firms had been hired to investigate and audit CONASUPO—precisely when the first investigative committee had been created. Only two years later, the Chamber had to retain two new accounting firms to analyze the same information and to review the operations of the same company.

The CONASUPO Committees' story is open to various interpretations. On the positive side, the first committee was formed as an automatic response to the request of the minority, avoiding the legal and constitutional ambiguities and controversies that had previously characterized other attempts to create similar investigative bodies. In that sense, this case set a good precedent for future efforts to create investigative committees. Both committees also received extensive media coverage. Regardless of the final conclusions and results, the two CONASUPO Committees managed to broaden the political role and significance of the House as a body that had the power to oversee the executive branch.

The negative side of the CONASUPO case appears obvious. Resulting in the prosecution of only two mid-level officials, the investigation had not penetrated deeply enough to disclose the extent of the corruption within the company. Future investigations and sanctions were left to the discretion of authorities in the executive branch, who since then have brought legal action against only five other former CONASUPO officials. Raúl Salinas, the original reason for the first investigation, was not judged to be guilty in the first CONASUPO Committee's final report, and no member of the executive branch ever accused him of corruption associated with CONASUPO. It is no exaggeration to say that, in its final report, the first investigative committee openly abdicated its authority to fight CONASUPO's corruption. On 14 occasions the committee had requested that the executive branch conduct further investigations. Deputy Quintana considered it a shame that the committee's 10-month effort and expenditure of 1.6 million pesos had resulted only in the recommendation that the executive branch should conduct further investigation, when the decision to investigates CONASUPO had been made precisely because the executive branch had not investigated the case at all." To a certain extent, one can infer that PRI members did not want to actually fulfill their role as legislative overseers of the executive branch and decided that the least risky option was to leave the responsibility to the president himself. As for the second CONASUPO Committee, the opposition majority in the Chamber seems to have played a major role in pressuring PRI deputies to vote along with other parties to approve the committee's creation in October 1997.

Finally, in the process of the PRI's attempts to limit the investigative scope of the committee, the opposition acted irresponsibly on several occasions. Opposition members tended to disclose confidential information prematurely. Some even reported false information in order to attract public attention; but by doing so, they caused government officials to view the committee's entire operation with suspicion and anger. These officials were convinced that the opposition was exaggerating the findings of the CONASUPO Committees only to highlight the alleged corruption of the government. It seemed evident to them that committee members had conducted business along party lines rather than according to the committee's goals and interests: partisanship of every type had characterized the committee's operation, and that attitude and behavior had diminished the prestige of the committee and the perceived gravity of its work; it also biased the results. Ultimately, it was the combined strategic behavior of the PRI and the opposition that managed to limit the performance and the status of the two CONASUPO Investigative Committees.

Privatization of TELMEX

Teléfonos de México had been a state-owned telephone monopoly before it was privatized in 1990. In recent years, however, many questions have been raised about the transparency and impartiality of that sale. Some critics have even hypothesized that former president Carlos Salinas might have been behind Carlos Slim, the entrepreneur who won the bid to purchase TELMEX.

In October 1996, PRD Deputy Anselmo Cruz requested that an investigative committee be formed to review the privatization process of TELMEX. In particular, he argued that TELMEX had been sold for $7.3 billion when the price was actually $30 billion. In that way, the privatization was seen as "a loss of U.S. $22.7 billion to the nation," because TELMEX was a public enterprise "owned by the people of Mexico."[55] Cruz's request was signed by 137 deputies (27.4 percent), only one of whom was a member of the PRI, and it was sent to the *Comisión de Régimen Interno* for its opinion. The investigative committee was never formed.[56]

The Mexican Institute for Social Security

On April 6, 1998, 164 deputies requested and received approval for the formation of an investigative committee to review the functioning of the Mexican Institute for Social Security (IMSS).[57] The committee's objectives were (1) to investigate the implications of a loan provided by the World Bank to fund investment spending within the IMSS, (2) to assess the functioning of the IMSS since 1973, (3) to analyze the "structural reforms" carried out by the institute since 1994, and (4) to promote reforms designed to strengthen Mexico's social security system. Some PRD deputies believed that the World Bank's loan contained a hidden agenda: to privatize the social security system in Mexico, a process that had begun, according to these deputies, when the pension system was reformed in the early 1990s. The IMSS provided ample information to the investigative committee; but, in the words of PAN Congressman Adame, the information provided was "*pura paja*." To avoid analysis of the information along political lines, the *Centro de Investigación y Docencia Económicas* (CIDE), a respected research center in Mexico City, was asked to assess the methodology used to analyze the information provided by the IMSS. CIDE concluded that there were many shortcomings in the IMSS's operation, especially in areas related to medical services, medical supplies, and administrative procedures. Nevertheless, the research center also concluded that the IMSS was already implementing various programs designed to overcome these shortcomings through its adoption of the Total Quality Program (*Plan Integral de Calidad*) and Institutional Medical Supply System (*Sistema de Abasto Institucional*).

The investigative committee was asked to present its final report before the legislature adjourned in August 2000. However, many committee members' political motivations, lack of interest and experience, and limited knowledge of the subject under investigation increase the likelihood that the results arising from this committee's work will contribute very little to strengthening the social security system in Mexico.

Financial Operations of the Federal Electricity Commission and *Luz y Fuerza del Centro*

In February 1999, President Zedillo proposed to submit a bill to Congress that was designed to modernize the electrical power sector in Mexico, including the privatization of state-owned power plants managed by the Federal Electricity Commission and *Luz y Fuerza del Centro* (LFC). A central argument contained in the president's bill was that the government lacked the financial resources required to modernize existing power plants and to construct new generation capacity in the future. According to the government, increasing the power capacity that the country will demand in the future would cost $25 billion, an amount that exceeded the financial resources of the republic, whose priority was social development not the operation of utility companies.

The bill was sent to Congress in March 1999, and many voices were immediately raised criticizing the government for selling "the assets of the people of Mexico." As part of this debate, on March 29, 1999, Deputies Lilia Reyes (PRI) and Cuauhtémoc Velasco (PRD) requested the formation of an investigative committee to review the financial operations of CFE and LFC and to assess the financial requirements actually needed to increase the companies' generation capacity. According to deputies, they needed this firsthand information to learn about the issue and to help them analyze the president's bill. The creation of the investigative committee was approved on April 15, 1999, and its term was set for a period of up to six months, with the possibility of extension if needed.[58] The committee was to have produced results by October 29, 1999, but it failed to do so. In early 2000, the committee was still working to reach consensus on a draft of a final report. At the end of 1999, for example, José Herrán, the committee chair at the time, encouraged its members to complete their investigation and to submit their conclusions. He was incapable of mustering enough support to achieve this goal, however. Despite the economic and social impact of CFE and LFC in the country's development, the investigative committee apparently has not contributed to their modernization.

Nacional Financiera's Pension Plan

On November 23, 1999, Independent Congress member Marcelo Ebrard requested the creation of a committee to investigate the pension plans of high-level functionaries at *Nacional Financiera*, a state-owned development bank in Mexico. Ebrard was interested in finding out how pensions were conferred as well as the names and amounts allocated both to the high-ranking officers formerly employed at the bank and to their relatives.[59] All the parliamentary groups, with the exception of the PRI, supported this request, and the investigative committee—consisting of seven deputies (three from the PRI and four from the opposition)[60]—was established on November 25, 1999.

The committee had its origin when Minister of Finance Angel Gurría appeared before the Chamber of Deputies on November 16, 1999, to present the budget bill. That day, Congressman Ebrard publicly accused Minister Gurría of receiving a second salary from an illegal retirement annuity from *Nacional Financiera*, the bank where Mr. Gurría had served as chief executive officer in the early 1990s. According to Mr. Ebrard, Minister Gurría had used his privileged position to negotiate a special retirement plan from the bank, despite the fact that he had not fulfilled the term of service required for eligibility. The accusations found fertile soil in a society already uncomfortable about this issue and exploded when it became evident that other former employees in the financial sector were also receiving allegedly illegal pensions.[61,2]

Amidst this atmosphere of criticisms and denunciations, an investigative committee was created with a mandate to produce a report by December 15, 1999. The committee published its report on the due date and concluded that "the retirement plans of both ministers, Angel Gurría and Oscar Espinosa Villarreal, were illegal." The report, approved by the opposition and rejected by the PRI, was sent to the executive branch for its decision on "whether to follow up or reject the results of the legislative investigation." Once the results became known, the Finance Ministry defended Mr. Gurría's honesty and reiterated its opinion that his retirement annuity was completely legal. The ministry also noted that "it is unfortunate that the committee's members from the PAN and the PRD have used the investigation as a tool to weaken the position of the man in charge of public finances in Mexico."[62] Regardless of the fairness and accuracy of the accusations from both sides, this committee proved to be effective in increasing the accountability of top government officials.

This chapter has described in detail several instances of legislative oversight as well as their lackluster results. The following three chapters will explore some possible systemic reasons behind the weakness of congressional oversight in Mexico.

Notes

[1] Political Constitution of the United Mexican States, 1994 (translated by the Federal Electoral Institute).

[2] To achieve that objective, different rules were modified. New parties were permitted to exist, as was the case with the Mexican Communist Party, which had been banned from the political arena for many years. Minority representation within Congress was strengthened by the introduction of a mixed electoral system, by which 100 out of the 400 Chamber seats were to be assigned only to opposition parties via a system of proportional representation. The rest of the House would be elected by the traditional plurality system. This formula operated from 1979 to 1988; thereafter, the mixed system underwent variations, and the Chamber membership increased to 500 deputies.

[3] It is important to recall that the 1977 political reform introduced the system by which 100 seats—25 percent of the House—were assigned to opposition party members by proportional representation and were exclusively reserved for the opposition, whose presence could be higher as their candidates were able to win a plurality of seats.

[4] It is interesting to note that the original proposal, as submitted by the executive branch, established a minimum threshold of one-third of deputies needed to request the formation of an investigative committee, instead of the

one-fourth finally approved. The reduction in the percentage was requested by Armando Labra and Miguel Montes, both PRI members, and was unanimously approved (see *Diary of Debates*, October 24, 1977).

[5] In 1974, reports from chiefs of administrative agencies were added to this requirement.

[6] The reform was enacted on January 31, 1974. In 1994, the attorney general of the republic was included in the list (see Sergio Elías Gutiérrez and Roberto Rives, *La Constitución Mexicana al final del siglo XX*, 2nd ed. (Mexico City: Las Líneas del Mar, S.A. de C.V., 1995), p. 329.

[7] See Jacques Rogozinski and Francisco J. Casas, "The Restructuring Process in Mexico," in *Public Administration in Mexico Today*, comp. María E. Vázquez Nava (Mexico City: Secretaría de la Contraloría de la Federación and Fondo de Cultura Económica, 1993); and Ignacio Pichardo Pagaza, *Ley Orgánica de la Administración Pública Federal*.

[8] Cecilia J. Mora-Donatto, *Las Comisiones parlamentarias de investigación como órganos de control político* (Mexico City: Cámara de Diputados and Universidad Nacional Autónoma de México, 1998), pp. 238–39.

[9] On April 8, 1999, Mexico's Green Party, led by Deputy Jorge Alejandro Jiménez, proposed reforming Article 93 to allow investigative committees to audit and investigate "any issue of relevance to the public interest falling under federal purview." The proposal also suggested changes to the congressional law that regulates the composition and operation of these committees (see Cámara de Diputados, *Gaceta Parlamentaria*, April 8, 1999).

[10] This proposal was made by Jorge Garabito, a PAN legislator. Armando Labra (PRI) criticized this position on the basis that it would give minorities decision power over majorities, something that would contradict the majority principle by which the House operates (see *Diary of Debates*, October 24, 1977).

[11] *Proceso*, a Mexican political weekly, played a central role in making public the accusations and evidence of telephone tapping in 1979 (see *Proceso*, nos. 153, 154, 155, and 156).

[12] The *Gran Comisión* used to be the most important House committee (see Nacif-Hernández, "The Mexican Chamber of Deputies").

[13] The PRI members were Juan Sabines (chair), Manuel Rangel Escamilla, Jesús Murillo Karam, and Rodolfo Alvarado Hernández; opposition members included Pablo Gómez (PCM), Hiram Escudero (PAN), and Hugo Amadeo González (PST).

[14] *Diary of Debates*, March 28, 1980.

[15] *Proceso*, April 7, 1980, p. 24.

[16] Gómez might have been referring to mid-level officials, since the first and second paragraphs of Article 93 do give authority to Congress to summon and request information from secretaries of state (ministers) and heads of administrative departments. Otherwise, his statement was incorrect.

[17] *Proceso*, April 7, 1980, pp. 24–25.

[18] Only the weekly *Proceso* regularly reported the activities of this committee. As for newspapers, *Uno Más Uno*, a major daily at that time, published only one very short article (January 28, 1980) about the committee during its four-month existence.

[19] As part of a new law to increase the effectiveness of the fight against organized crime, as of 1995 telephone tapping was legislated and permitted under certain circumstances.

[20] Requested on October 11, 1988.

[21] *Diary of Debates*, October 18, 1988.

[22] Even though the investigative committee was never created, other legislative bodies did perform some sort of supervisory function regarding *Laguna Verde*. The Energy Committee of the Chamber of Deputies held hearings with officials from the Ministry of Energy and from the Federal Electricity Commission, and some members of that committee visited the installations at the nuclear power plant. The Ecology Committee also took part in these activities. But these committees had neither the status nor the authority that an investigative committee would have had.

[23] This case was linked to the PEMEX case. Indeed, BANPESCA's authorities were accused of having financed the acquisition of two oil tankers that had been rented to PEMEX in 1985, something anomalous for BANPESCA, whose credits were supposed to be used for fishing development and ports, rather than for oil-related businesses (see *La Jornada*, April 13, 1990).

[24] Information derived from personal interviews with Jesús Ramón Rojo (PAN) and Trinidad Lanz (PRI), as well as from the *Diary of Debates* (February and April 1990) and newspapers (*Uno Más Uno* and *La Jornada*).

[25] Jesús Ortega (PRD), *Diary of Debates*, April 24, 1990.

[26] *Diary of Debates*, April 24, 1990.

[27] As stated by the minister of the treasury on May 5, 1990 (*La Jornada*) and by Ricardo Olivares (PRI) (see *Diary of Debates*, July 1990).

[28] Jesús Ortega, *Diary of Debates*, July 1990.

[29] As exemplified by Ricardo Olivares (PRI), ibid.

[30] Personal interviews with Jesús Ramón Rojo and Astolfo Vicencio Tovar, both from the PAN.

[31] According to a member of the BANPESCA Committee, Astolfo Vicencio Tovar (PAN), "the illegitimacy and weakness of President Salinas made the PRI parliamentary group vulnerable to the strength of the opposition in Congress." Thus, the PRI could hardly avoid the creation of the BANPESCA Committee (personal interview, February 22, 1996.)

[32] *Diary of Debates*, December 28, 1989.

[33] The request had originally been drafted on December 28, 1989, but it could not be presented to the floor due to an overloaded legislative agenda (ibid., December 28, 1989, and March 14, 1990).

[34] Abel Vicencio Tovar (PAN), *Diary of Debates*, April 30, 1991.

[35] Juan N. Guerra (PRD), ibid.

[36] Argument made by Juan N. Guerra, ibid., May 8, 1991.

[37] *Uno Más Uno*, June 28, 1991.

[38] The attorney general, Fernando Antonio Lozano Gracia (PAN), was appointed by President Ernesto Zedillo to give credibility to the investigations of political assassinations committed during the previous year—those of PRI presidential candidate Luis D. Colosio and José F. Ruiz Massieu. It was assumed that an opposition member would face fewer obstacles in trying to solve these cases. However, time proved that the inexperience of this official was also an obstacle to combating corruption.

[39] *Diary of Debates*, November 28, 1995.

[40] This committee was created in 1994 to function as a bargaining table among the leaders of the parliamentary groups.

[41] The members were Manuel Hinojosa (chair, PRI), Javier Gutiérrez Vidal (PAN), Alfonso Reyes Medrano (PRI), Joaquín Vela (PT), Víctor Quintana (PRD), Adolfo Aguilar Zínser (Independent), Carlos Navarrete Ruiz (PRD), Jesús Ramón Rojo (PAN), José Luis Salcedo (PRI), Manuel Bersitáin (PAN), Carlos Rubén Calderón (PRI), Fernando Salgado (PRI), Ignacio González Rebolledo (PRI), Jorge Cejudo Díaz (PRI), Juan Manuel Cruz Acevedo (PRI), and Jesús Rodríguez y Rodríguez (PRI) (see *Diary of Debates*, November 30, 1995).

[42] The main political personages accused were Jaime Serra (former minister of commerce), Julio César Ruiz Ferro (governor of the State of Chiapas), Javier Bonilla (minister of labor), and Carlos Salinas (former president of Mexico). All of them, in some way or another, had had some contact with CONASUPO's operations at some point during 1982–92.

[43] This unofficial charge was made by Independent Congressman Adolfo Aguilar Zínser, but was quickly dismissed for lack of legal basis or proof. Indeed, an outside accounting firm conducted an audit and concluded that the

payments made by CONASUPO to MASECA—authorized by Ernesto Zedillo, who was the minister of planning and budget at the time—were legal and had been previously authorized by the Chamber of Deputies itself (see *Uno Más Uno*, July 18, 1996).

[44] *La Jornada*, January 25, 1996.

[45] The first three archives the committee received from CONASUPO at the beginning of its investigation contained 95 million pages of documents and billions of pieces of electronic data (see *Reforma*, January 10, 1996).

[46] *El Financiero*, May 31, 1996.

[47] According to two PRI deputies, the leader of the PRI parliamentary group, Humberto Roque, asked his colleagues to close the CONASUPO case and adjourn the committee as soon as possible to avoid further damage to the image of both the president and the party (see *La Jornada*, September 4, 1996).

[48] These were the payments authorized by Ernesto Zedillo, the minister of planning and budget at the time.

[49] This information was derived from comments made by various deputies between September 27 and October 6, 1996 (see *La Jornada* and *Uno Más Uno*).

[50] Curiously, four days after the committee adjourned, the minister of the comptrollership initiated legal action against a few former officials of CONASUPO: Salvador Giordano, Juan Manuel Pasalagua (who had already been mentioned as legally guilty in the committee's final report), Carlos Alamán Bueno, Víctor Gómez, Marco Antonio Bareño Arvizu, and Agustín Vargas Durán, all of whom (except for Giordano) were mid-level bureaucrats within CONASUPO.

[51] See *Proceso*, September 29, 1996.

[52] The members of the second CONASUPO Committee included Enrique Jackson and Jaime Talancón from the PRI; Miguel Raya and Alberto López from the PRD; Margarita Pérez Gavilán and Abelardo Perales from the PAN; Miguel Garza and Verónica Velasco from the PVEM; and Juan José Cruz and José Luis López from the PT.

[53] For example, PRI Deputy Ricardo Monreal (today a PRD member and governor of Zacatecas) said that his party did not oppose the reopening of the CONASUPO Committee, but that approval required a clear regulation as to how such committees should be formed and the rules under which they would operate (see *Diary of Debates*, October 30, 1997).

[54] The accounting firm calculated the monetary damage to be 9,162 million pesos, the equivalent of approximately $916 million at an exchange rate of 10

pesos per U.S. dollar, which was the market rate in February 1999 (see *Excélsior* and other major newspapers, January 28, 1999).

[55] *Diary of Debates,* October 10, 1996.

[56] According to a major newspaper, as soon as the request was made on the floor, the leader of the PRI parliamentary group, Humberto Roque, asked for time before making his decision so that he could discuss the case with the president (see *La Jornada,* October 11, 1996).

[57] The members of the committee were Víctor Manuel Carreto, Jorge Estefán, José Antonio Estefan, Guillermo Barnés, Domingo Yorio, Vicente de la Cruz, and Alfredo Phillips, all from the PRI; Santiago Padilla, Jorge Silva, Ricardo García Sáinz, and Gonzalo Rojas from the PRD; Marco Adame, Gustavo Espinosa, Gustavo Vicencio, and Jesús Montejo from the PAN; and Mercedes Maciel from the PT.

[58] The members of this committee were Guillermo Barnés, Víctor Manuel Carreto, Charbel Jorge Estefan, Marco Antonio Fernández, Fernando Gómez Esparsa, Catalina Herrera Díaz, Francisco Javier Santillán, and Domingo Yorio Saqui from the PRI; Martín Contreras Rivera, José Herrán Cabrera, Arturo Ontiveros, and Juan José Rodríguez Pratts from the PAN; Jesús Martín del Campo, Benito Osorio Romero, Luis Rojas Chávez, and Cuauhtémoc Velasco from the PRD; Juan Cruz Martínez from the PT; and Alejandro Jiménez Taboada from the PVEM.

[59] See *Diary of Debates,* November 23, 1999.

[60] The members of this committee were Jorge Estefan Chidiac, Miguel Sadot Sánchez, and Alberto Curi Naime from the PRI; Ramón María Nava and Edgar Ramírez from the PAN; and Alberto López Rosas and Jesús Martín del Campo from the PRD. The deputy who requested the creation of the committee, Marcelo Ebrard, is noticeably absent; he did not join the committee because of PRI opposition.

[61] One such case was that of the minister of tourism, Oscar Espinosa Villarreal.

[62] Ministry of Finance press release, December 14, 1999.

CHAPTER FOUR

THE INSTITUTION OF NONCONSECUTIVE REELECTION

THE POSSIBILITY OF REELECTION IS A MAIN INGREDIENT IN THE LOGIC of parliamentary politics; it is a visible and common incentive faced by legislators and one that shapes their behavior if they want to be reelected.[1] Today, the institution of reelection is widespread, with the rare exceptions of Mexico and Costa Rica.[2] In Mexico, reelection to consecutive terms of office is prohibited, but reelection after an intervening period is permitted. (Costa Rica's Constitution establishes that deputies cannot be reelected to successive terms.) During a visit to Mexico a few years ago, the Italian political scientist Giovanni Sartori called this restriction the "*extravaganza mexicana*." In his opinion, Mexican politics was turned upside down, because legislators—unable to stand for reelection—were missing the rewards that are derived from a job well done. According to Sartori, no political organization can perform effectively if it lacks the rewards needed to foster good performance.[3] The Mexican Congress is a case in point—the absence of incentives has weakened its autonomy and limited its members' professionalism.

In Mexico, consecutive reelection was prohibited starting in 1933, and this institutional change has had profound consequences on the behavior, profile, and strategies for career advancement of members of Congress. These behavioral consequences have affected the way Congress operates and interacts with the executive branch. In particular, this chapter tries to answer the following questions:

1. How has the institution of nonconsecutive reelection impeded deputies' experience and professionalism?

2. How has the institution of nonconsecutive reelection shaped and affected the goals and behavior of Mexican legislators?

3. How has the institution of nonconsecutive reelection reversed the direction of political accountability of Mexican legislators?

4. How has the behavior resulting from this institution affected the general relationship between the executive and the legislative branches of government, and in particular, the way Congress oversees public finances in Mexico?

CONSTITUTIONAL FOUNDATION: ARTICLE 59

The institution of nonconsecutive reelection refers to the provision contained in Article 59 of the 1917 Constitution, which prohibits the reelection of legislators to consecutive terms of office, even though they can be reelected after an intervening full term. The text of Article 59 is as follows:

> Article 59. Senators and deputies to the Congress of the Union cannot be re-elected for the immediately following term.
>
> Alternate senators and deputies may be elected for the immediately following term as full senators and deputies, provided that they have not served [in the office of their principals]; but titular [full] senators and deputies cannot be elected for the immediately following term in the capacity of alternates [*sic*].

The nonconsecutive reelection clause was established in 1933 as a result of a bill introduced by the *Partido Nacional Revolucionario* (PNR), the forerunner of today's Institutional Revolutionary Party. The reform was aimed at banning the reelection of presidents and state governors as well as prohibiting consecutive reelection of senators, federal deputies, state legislators, and mayors (*presidentes municipales*), all of whom, according to this provision, can be reelected to the same office after at least one intervening period has elapsed.[4] After intense debate in November and December 1932,

Congress passed the initiative and sent the bill to state legislatures for approval. On April 29, 1933, the reforms banning consecutive reelection were promulgated and took legal effect.[5] This institutional reform would prove to have a lasting and significant effect in shaping relations between the executive and legislative branches of government in Mexico, as will be detailed in the sections that follow. The restriction "transformed Mexican politics into what can be described as a regular 'game of musical chairs,' thereby affecting the operation of every single office at federal, state and municipal levels, and re-structuring the patterns of political careers."[6]

One of the main arguments offered by proponents of the *antireeleccionista* reform was that it would avoid *continuismo* and the formation of political enclaves within the national Congress, state governments, and local legislatures. According to some of the proponents, the nonreelection clause would bring a new generation of young politicians into national political life and would therefore enhance a healthy circulation of elites.[7] However, other, less-visible factors might have been behind these reform proposals. According to both Arnaut and Marván, the constitutional reform that led to barring consecutive reelection was a component of the PNR National Committee's global strategy to consolidate its power nationally and across regions.[8]

Founded in 1929 by Plutarco Elías Calles, the PNR was designed to bring political stability and peace to a country that had suffered from political turmoil, coup d'états, political violence, and assassinations. *Caudillismo* needed to be replaced, in Calles's words, by institutions, and one of the ways to attack *personalismo* in Mexican politics was to reduce the political leverage of local *caciques*. Party officials believed that banning reelection would help in that effort, because local bosses were able to protect their political clout and resources by supporting and financing the reelection of their allies, mostly local deputies. Therefore, according to this rationale, if reelection were forbidden, *caciques* would lose political leverage and influence at the local level. According to Jeffrey Weldon, state legislatures were powerful within this network of local interests, because local legislatures had vast powers vis-à-vis not only *ayuntamientos* but also state governments. "[S]tate legislatures after the Revolution were the center of local politics, the main resource of the local parties and their machines.... In these circumstances, there could be good arguments for prohibiting the re-election of local deputies (if the aim was to change the *foci* of political power from *caciques* and local parties to the PNR National Committee)....[T]he state legislature was the keystone to understanding a political machine—not the public administration of the state or municipal governments. Though the jobs and money were to be found in the state or municipal governments, it was in the legislatures that the political power resided."[9]

Because local legislatures and *caciques* were the greatest threats to the PNR's national goals, it seems plausible that banning consecutive reelection was aimed more at limiting political opportunities for local deputies, rather than doing so for federal senators and deputies, who posed no challenge to the PNR National Committee. However, an antireelectionist reform had to encompass all elective offices in order to avoid the perception that the reform had a specific target and thus reveal the real motives behind it.

The prohibition of consecutive reelection contributed in a very important way to the concentration of power at the national level and, even though the power of local bosses was not always diminished, they gradually began to use it to support the national party rather than local legislatures or parties. For Nacif-Hernández, "the no re-election constitutional amendments allowed the PNR to build a comprehensive system of office rotation which put powerful weapons to punish and reward individual politicians in the hands of the national leadership. Office holders became completely vulnerable; they became entirely dependent on the most extensive existing mechanism of political promotion—the PNR.... [Because the party became central to politicians' strategies to continue and advance their careers, such incentives] reinforced the role, and therefore the power, of the PNR's national organization.... [In this context], local parties and constituency-oriented electoral organizations became of extremely limited political use."[10]

In 1964, the Chamber made a serious attempt to restore consecutive reelection when it approved a constitutional amendment to Article 59, which allowed consecutive reelection of federal deputies. Proponents of the reform claimed that the move would strengthen Congress, increase the representativeness of legislators, and stimulate a more qualified and experienced cadre of deputies. Despite gaining consensus in the House, the bill was unanimously rejected when it reached the Senate. Opponents inaccurately, but effectively, argued that the amendment was contrary to the spirit of the Mexican revolution, whose main slogan had been a reflection of one of the initial demands of that historical revolt (*Sufragio Efectivo, No Reelección*).[11] The argument against the bill was inaccurate, because the target of the *Maderista* revolution's and the 1917 Constitution's antireelection demand was the presidency, not Congress. However, it was an effective strategy because the collective memory of Porfirio Diaz's more than 30-year rule had a very negative impact on public opinion, which continues to this day.

Today, it is reasonable to state that, after 67 years of existence, the institution of nonconsecutive reelection has atrophied not only the functioning of state legislatures but also the oversight capabilities and functioning of the national Congress, as the following sections will explain. The result—a weak legislative branch of government that is subsumed under a powerful and all-encompassing executive branch—gave way to the golden era of Mexican presidentialism.[12]

THE IMPACT OF NONCONSECUTIVE REELECTION ON DEPUTIES' EXPERIENCE, SPECIALIZATION, AND PROFESSIONALISM

Nonconsecutive reelection affects the professionalism and experience of Mexican deputies. In particular, nonreelectability results in the limited legislative experience of deputies, lack of specialization in oversight activities, and a low level of professionalism. These three characteristics are an intrinsic part of today's Mexican Congress and account for much of the inability of the legislative branch to adequately oversee the executive branch.

Table 4.1
Percentage of Deputies Reelected to Office, 1970–97[a]

Legislative Term	Percentage
1970–73	12.7
1973–76	14.7
1976–79	16.2
1979–82	17.8
1982–85	13.9
1985–88	22.0
1988–91	21.6
1991–94	16.9
1994–97	18.0
Average	**17.5**

[a] After at least one interim period, as stated in the Constitution.

Source: Emma Campos, "Un Congreso sin congresistas: La No-Reelección consecutiva en el Poder Legislativo mexicano, 1934-1997" (B.A. thesis, Instituto Tecnológico Autónomo de México, 1996), p. 55.

Insufficient Legislative Experience

Every three years the Chamber is required to reinvent itself: 500 deputies leave office searching for new jobs and 500 new deputies enter a new business with which most have never had any previous direct contact or experience. Although reelection is permitted after an intervening full term, most deputies in each legislature have never been deputies before. As table 4.1 shows, between 1970 and 1997, an average of only 17.5 percent of incoming deputies had previous Chamber experience. In other words, of the 3,381 deputies who served in the Chamber over this period, only 593 had had previous experience. The remainder—more than 80 percent—had very little knowledge of the business in which the Chamber was engaged.[13]

By hindering the possibility of building long-term legislative careers, nonreelectability discourages talented and ambitious politicians, because they do not consider the Chamber to be an attractive

Table 4.2
Impact of Nonconsecutive Reelection on Deputies' Professionalism
(as perceived by deputies)[a]
(N = 49)

Degree	Percentage
Much	87.5
Little	8.3
Nothing	4.1

[a] Question asked of deputies: Many have suggested that the principle of nonconsecutive reelection in the legislative branch limits the professionalism of federal deputies in Mexico. How much do you agree with this statement?

Source: Personal interviews.

vehicle for initiating or consolidating their political careers. As table 4.2 shows, according to 87 percent of the deputies interviewed, nonreelectability had substantially limited the professionalism or expertise of federal deputies in Mexico; 8 percent believed it had little impact; and only 4 percent thought that the nonreelection clause had not affected deputies' level of professionalism and competence.

Lack of Specialization in Oversight Activities

To make matters worse, only a very small fraction of incoming deputies with prior House experience specialize in oversight activities. Most reelected deputies join different committees when they enter the Chamber for a second or third time, and the expertise they had acquired in previous legislatures is lost. Of the 350 deputies who served on the Supervisory Committee between 1920 and 1997, only 7 served on it twice (a minuscule 2 percent) and only one was on this committee three times (0.3 percent).[14] If specialization is defined narrowly—that is, that three full terms are required to become knowledgeable about oversight—then only 0.3 percent of the deputies over the period 1920–97 were specialized in this area. If the definition is brought down to the lowest threshold—two terms of related experience—then the figure rises to a still modest 2 percent.

Table 4.3
Deputies' Specialization in Committee Work, 1970–94
(number of times serving on the same committee)

Committee	Number of Members	One-Term Members	Two-Term Members	Three-Term Members	More than Three Terms
Budget	314 (100%)	294 (93.6%)	20 (6.4%)	0 (0.0%)	0 (0%)
Gobernación	313 (100%)	291 (93.0%)	19 (6.0%)	3 (1.0%)	0 (0%)
Supervisory (1920–97)	350 (100%)	342 (97.7%)	7 (2.0%)	1 (0.3%)	0 (0%)

Sources: Diary of Debates, various years; Congresssional Records, various years; Diccionario biográfico del gobierno mexicano, various years.

The situation was no better for the Budget Committee: only 6.4 percent of the committee members served on it twice, and none served three times. The same pattern can be observed with the *Gobernación* Committee, a congressional body with no oversight responsibilities. These results are broken down in table 4.3.

Lack of specialization among members of the Supervisory Committee was a result of two factors. First, there were no incentives to become specialized. If career advancement for PRI members was not attached to their performance on committees (but to accountability to the presidency, as discussed in chapter 5 of this book), then there was no reason to devote the resources needed to become knowledgeable in the complex duty of overseeing public finances.[15] Second, over the period of this study, the Supervisory Committee has not traditionally been among the most visible and politically attractive committees. Only recently has this committee emerged as a key player in congressional politics, probably as a result of the chair being occupied by an opposition deputy since 1994.[16] The deputies interviewed considered the *Gobernación*, Treasury, and Budget Committees to be more important. (Their responses are shown in table 4.4.) Obviously, then, legislators tended to devote more of their attention and efforts to the agenda of these committees than to that of the Supervisory Committee. Nevertheless, as this committee acquires more authority, resources, and visibility, it will become more attractive to members of Congress in the 58th Legislature as well as in future legislatures.

Low Professional Quality

According to personal interviews, almost 45 percent of current and former deputies believed that the professional quality of deputies was "average"; 30 percent considered it to be "low"; and only 18 percent evaluated it as "high." (See table 4.5.) When aggregated, this yields a score of 5.6 on a scale of 1–10.

Nonreelectability contributed to deputies' low level of professionalism, because it minimized the rewards arising out of careers in the legislature in comparison with those in the government bureaucracy. By prohibiting reelection, the Mexican Congress was not able

Table 4.4
Most Important Committees
(as perceived by deputies)[a]
(*N* = 49)

Committee	Number of Positive Responses
Gobernación	40
Hacienda	26
Budget	22
Supervisory	15
Justice	11
Other[b]	9

[a] Question asked of deputies: Of all the House committees, which have been the most important?
[b] Foreign Relations, Energy, Commerce, and Federal District.
Source: Personal interviews.

Table 4.5
Professional Quality of Deputies, 1994–97
(as perceived by current and former deputies)[a]
(*N* = 49)

Level of Qualification	Percentage
Very high	2.0
High	18.3
Average	44.8
Low	30.6
Very low	2.0
Weighted grade (Scale 1–10)[b]	5.6

[a] Question asked of deputies: Deputies' professional quality varies by parliamentary group. If you had to assign an average grade to deputies in today's legislature (56th, 1994–97), how would you grade their average professional quality?
[b] Very high = 10; high = 8; average = 6; low = 4; very low = 2.
Source: Personal interviews.

to provide attractive political rewards for politicians trying to build political careers. In contrast, the executive branch was able to offer more options. The facts speak for themselves. Over the past 30 years, careers in the federal bureaucracy, especially in the planning and financial sectors, were more profitable and rewarding than careers within the electoral and legislative arenas. For example, the last five presidents—from Luis Echeverria (1970–76) to Ernesto Zedillo (1994–2000)—climbed to the top almost exclusively via the echelons of the federal bureaucracy. Consequently, the government bureaucracy tended to attract the most talented people, while the legislative branch tended to get politicians who were less qualified.[17] This recruiting pattern meant that government officials were, in general, more competent and qualified than legislators, causing an asymmetry of human capital that hindered Congress's ability to balance the executive branch.

Deputies themselves shared this view, as the responses shown in table 4.6 demonstrate. A majority—55 percent—believed that "officials are more competent than deputies"; 24 percent thought that "officials and deputies are about the same" in terms of professional quality; and only 6 percent perceived that "deputies are more competent."

The recruitment of more talented people into the central bureaucracy is a result of political rewards offered by both branches of government. Since Congress is becoming a more important player in Mexican politics, it is also becoming a more attractive route to political advancement. In addition, as elected office and political experience have come to be considered valuable assets for nomination to the presidency and other offices, it is very likely that many ambitious political aspirants will choose a term in Congress as a way to begin their political careers, thus balancing bureaucrats' and legislators' competence levels. The July 2000 presidential election sent a signal to the political marketplace: the three major candidates—Vicente Fox of the National Action Party, Francisco Labastida of the PRI, and Cuauhtemoc Cárdenas of the Democratic Revolutionary Party— had all held elected offices in the past. Fox himself began his political career by winning a seat in the Chamber of Deputies in 1988, where he served until 1991.

Table 4.6
**Comparison of Professional Quality of Deputies
with Government Officials**
(as perceived by deputies)[a] (in percent)
(N = 49)

Response	Opinions by Party			Total
	PRI	PAN	PRD	
Officials are more competent	55.5	38.4	77.7	55.1
Officials and deputies are about the same	22.2	38.4	11.1	24.4
Deputies are more competent	3.7	7.6	11.1	6.1
Inappropriate comparison	18.5	15.3	0.0	14.2

[a] Question asked of deputies: In general, how do you compare the professional quality of high-ranking officials in the federal government (administration) with that of federal deputies?
Source: Personal interviews.

THE IMPACT OF NONCONSECUTIVE REELECTION ON DEPUTIES' MOTIVATIONS AND GOALS

Having established how the institution of nonconsecutive reelection affected the profile of Mexican legislators—their experience, specialization, and professionalism—it is now possible to analyze how nonreelectability affected deputies' goals and strategies for career advancement. The transformation occurred through a complex process whereby outgoing deputies, prohibited from remaining in office, sought higher office and adapted their behavior so that they could be elected to party candidacies that were determined by the president. By "forcing" deputies to leave office after serving a full term, nonconsecutive reelection discouraged "static ambition"— that is, a politician's desire to make a long career out of a particular office—and fostered "progressive ambition," as deputies aspired (and some felt compelled) to attain higher office.[18] In that way, the House became a "temporary station" in the career paths of Mexican politicians, never a professional end in itself.[19] As a result, when the legislature adjourned, outgoing deputies faced several options for continuing their political careers. The range and number of options "potentially" available to outgoing legislators are referred to as "the structure of opportunities."[20] Typically, between 1970 and 1999, this structure consisted of the offices that are outlined in figure 4.1 on page 110.[21]

Although career paths followed by PRI deputies over the last decades encompassed a wide variety of offices, not all offices were pursued or achieved at similar rates. Over the period of study, some offices were considered more important than others as subsequent career paths for federal deputies. These include Senate seats and governorships, followed by party positions. The federal government ranks low on this list.[22]

Of all the senators who served between 1982 and 1994, almost 68 percent had been federal deputies at least once prior to their arrival in the upper house, and 33 percent became senators immediately after leaving the Chamber. The numbers shown in table 4.7 place the Senate as an obvious career path for outgoing deputies and show that experience as a deputy is an asset when seeking a Senate seat in the subsequent term. The next logical step for outgoing PRI deputies was a governorship, as the table shows. Of all the governors who served between 1976 and 1995, approximately 52 percent had been federal deputies at least one time prior to their gubernatorial positions; 21 percent had been deputies just before becoming gubernatorial candidates.[23] The PRI structure was the third most attractive route for outgoing deputies. Between 1970 and 1997, of the 40 individuals who served as party leaders (president or secretary general), 7 (17.5 percent) had been federal deputies just prior to assuming their party leadership positions.

In contrast to these career paths, a position in the federal government was not a natural step for outgoing PRI deputies. Data available show that for 1984–92, an average of 6 percent of high-ranking officials had had some kind of experience in elective office (as federal or local deputies, senators, governors, or mayors). That means that the percentage of public servants with backgrounds as federal deputies is much lower than the 6 percent shown in table 4.7.[24] While the

Figure 4.1
Structure of Opportunities: Most Relevant Office Options for Outgoing PRI Deputies, 1970–99
(size of office indicated in parentheses)

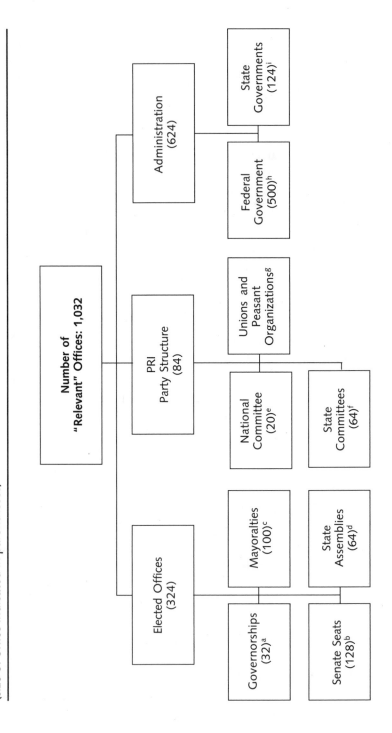

a Includes the chief of the government of Mexico City, who was first elected by direct vote in 1997.

b Today, the Mexican Senate is composed of 128 members, but for most of the period of study it had a membership of only 64 senators.

c As of August 2000, there were 2,419 *municipios* in Mexico. Their size and importance vary greatly—from small rural and poor *municipios* in the south to some *municipios* like Tlalnepantla, in the State of Mexico, which has a large concentration of industry and revenue. It is estimated that approximately 100 *municipios* actually deserve political attention, either because they are state capitals (31) or because they are economically strong or have large populations.

d The total number of local deputies (there are no state senators) is 854, an average of 28 per state, not including Mexico City, which has had its own assembly only since 1988. Of this total, it is estimated that the only attractive offices are those of the Speaker and the second-ranking deputy in each of the 31 state assemblies.

e The size of the PRI National Committee has varied over time; the number given here is an average. Federal deputies frequently assume party positions while still in office.

f The PRI has 32 state committees. Only the presidency and the secretary general of each of them are considered attractive options for federal deputies.

g Unions affiliated with the Mexican Workers Confederation (CTM) constitute the axis of the workers' sector within the PRI. Frequently, union leaders simultaneously hold legislative seats and remain union leaders after their House terms expire. As for the peasant organizations, the most attractive are those affiliated with the National Peasant Confederation, the basis of the PRI's peasant sector.

h The *Diccionario biográfico del gobierno mexicano* records 1,162 high-ranking officials in 1992 (from general director to secretary of state). That number includes the *paraestatal* sector (public enterprises and developmental agencies). A fraction of that figure—about 500—represents the number of attractive options.

i The *Diccionario* records 401 high-ranking state officials in 1992. It is estimated that, on average, only four posts per state are attractive to federal deputies (secretary general, treasury and finance secretary, secretary of economic development, and secretary of education).

Table 4.7
Predominant Career Paths of PRI Deputies, 1982–97

Structure of Opportunities	Size of Office[a]	Size of Relevant Options[a]	Holders of Offices Who Were Previously Deputies (%)			Predominant Path
			Period	Before	Just Before	
Elected Office	3,368	257				
Senate seats	64	64	1982–94	67.7[b]	33.1[b]	✓
Governorships	31	31	1976–95	52.4[b]	21.4[b]	✓
Mayoralties	2,419	100	—	—	—	
State assemblies	854	62	—	—	—	
Party Structure	84	84				
National Committee	20	20	1970–97	High[c]	17.5[d]	✓
Union and peasant organizations	?	?	1970–94	High	High[c]	✓
State committees	64	64	—	—	—	
Administration	1,563	624				
Federal government	1,162	500	1984–92	6.0 (max)[e]	—	
State governments	401	124	1992	30.4 (max)[e]	—	
Total	5,015	965				

Notes and Sources:
[a] See figure 4.1.
[b] See Benito Nacif-Hernández, "The Mexican Chamber of Deputies: The Political Significance of Non-Consecutive Re-election" (Ph.D. diss., Faculty of Social Studies, Oxford University, 1995), pp. 114–18, tables 3.3–3.6.
[c] No public records exist, but it is common for a high percentage of party members and union leaders to have previously been legislators or even to have held legislative seats simultaneously with party positions.
[d] Due to unavailability of relevant data, this includes only the two highest positions: the president and secretary general, occupied by 40 individuals in 1970–97 (see María Amparo Casar, "Los presidentes y secretarios generales del PRI," *Reforma* [Special Supplement: *Enfoque*], September 28, 1997).
[e] Average for the period. This number overestimates the actual figure, because it includes high-ranking officials who had previously held elected office but does not distinguish the type of office (senator, federal deputy, mayor, local deputy, and others). Therefore, it is estimated that the actual figure is much lower, perhaps by half in the case of the federal government (see *Diccionario biográfico*, 1984, 1987, 1989, and 1992).

Table 4.8
Deputies' Office Goals
(57th Legislature, 1997–2000)[a]
($N = 164$)

Office Goal	Percentage
Elected office	30
Social organizations	15
Private sector	13
Academia and research	11
State government	10
Party structure	8
Federal government	7
Other	4

[a] Question asked of deputies: Once your term as deputy is over, what is your next office goal?

Source: Reforma interviews.

road from the Chamber to the federal administration was quite narrow, it was wider for bureaucrats trying to pursue political careers. If only 6 percent of high-ranking officials had legislative background, as many as 71 percent of deputies had had experience in administrative positions.[25] Therefore, if "the Chamber of Deputies is not a strategic position to thrive as an administrative careerist, still it represents a significant outlet of ambition for administrative officials, as it constitutes a temporary station which may lead to the Senate, or the governorships of their home states."[26] All this information is summarized in table 4.7.

A survey asking deputies from the 57th Legislature (1997–2000) about their goals for subsequent office supports the argument that Senate seats, governorships, and party positions constitute the predominant paths for outgoing deputies' career advancement. (Their responses are shown as percentages in table 4.8.) Their primary goal—as indicated by 30 percent of the deputies interviewed—was elected office, either Senate seats or governorships.[27] Deputies' second goal was leadership in social organizations (basically unions,

Table 4.9
Deputies' Opinions About Legislative Reelection[a]
(57th Legislature, 1997–2000)
($N = 164$)

Statement	Percentage
Unlimited and consecutive reelection should exist	20
Consecutive reelection with term limits should be allowed	44
Nonconsecutive reelection is fine	22

[a] Question asked of deputies: Which of the following statements do you agree with the most?
Source: *Reforma* interviews.

nongovernmental organizations, and peasant organizations), as mentioned by 15 percent of the deputies surveyed. Another 8 percent aspired to positions within the party structure, and a low 7 percent gave the federal government as their choice for their next office. All these figures are quite similar to those inferred from data shown in table 4.7 and therefore reinforce the conclusion.

THE FUTURE OF LEGISLATIVE REELECTION

There is a growing consensus that the political wisdom of the 1930s—which gave rise to nonconsecutive reelection—no longer applies to present-day Mexico. As table 4.9 shows, according to 44 percent of deputies interviewed, "consecutive reelection with term limits should be allowed"; 22 percent believed that things were fine as they were (that is, nonconsecutive reelection); and 20 percent leaned toward the idea of allowing unlimited and consecutive reelection. The numbers, albeit with different modalities, totally support the idea of allowing some form of consecutive reelection.

Reinstating reelection would have a significant impact on legislative oversight, as the responses shown in table 4.10 demonstrate. Of the deputies interviewed, 66 percent believed that this institutional change would have a great impact on the quality and quantity of the

Table 4.10
Impact of Reinstating Reelection on the Increase
of Chamber Oversight of the Executive Branch
(as perceived by deputies)[a]
(*N* = 49)

Degree	Percentage
Much	66.6
Little	25.0
None	8.3

[a] Question asked of deputies: If deputies could run for consecutive reelection, do you think that the quantity and quality of legislative oversight of the executive branch would increase?
Source: Personal interviews.

Chamber's oversight; 25 percent considered it to be negligible; and only 8 percent thought that there would be no impact at all.

As this chapter has shown, a large number of current and former deputies believe that the institution of nonconsecutive reelection has contributed to the decrease in the effectiveness of congressional performance and to the erosion of Congress's autonomy. Nevertheless, some ideological opposition to the idea of reinstalling legislative reelection still exists.[28] Rational arguments alone cannot bring about this institutional change, as the 1964 attempt demonstrated. This issue will be propelled by a combination of good arguments, a permissive political environment, and the building of a political coalition. Increasingly, more voices have been heard expressing support for reinstituting consecutive reelection.[29]

Vicente Fox himself and his team have constantly stated that they plan to introduce a bill to restore consecutive reelection of federal deputies, senators, and *presidentes municipales* (mayors). During his first formal appearance as an official presidential candidate, Francisco Labastida, the PRI's unsuccessful candidate, also announced his intention to reinstate the reelection of deputies.[30] In addition, both the PRI and the PAN leadership in the newly installed 58th Legislature have proposed to restore consecutive reelection.

Given the legitimacy and political support that Fox enjoys, it is likely that his proposed legislation will be passed in time for members of the 59th Legislature (2003–2006) to run for reelection in 2006. Jorge Castañeda, a close adviser to Fox, said recently in Washington, D.C., that Fox would have liked the consecutive reelection bill to have been passed by the 57th Legislature, because Fox could have benefitted from a more autonomous and professional Congress—one whose members would be more accountable to the electorate and thus less tempted to be obstructionist. However, the 58th Legislature (2000–2003) will not be in a position to pass legislation that would enable its members to seek reelection and remain in office. If the new Congress is to pass such legislation, its members must not benefit from the reform; they must leave the option open for members of the subsequent legislature, who will take office in 2003.

Notes

[1] Maintaining power and seeking higher office appear to be driving forces among all politicians. Other goals may exist—such as shaping "good" public policy, helping the poor, or getting wealthy—but attaining, maintaining, and increasing political power do not contradict these other motives, and usually, the former motives complement and facilitate conditions for the achievement of the latter.

[2] Until 1996, Ecuador was another case where reelection was prohibited, but a constitutional reform lifted the ban in that year (see Béjar, "La Reelección parlamentaria en México," p. 32). Mexico and Costa Rica are the only countries where consecutive reelection is prohibited (see Careaga, "Reformas institucionales que fracasan").

[3] Personal interview, July 1996.

[4] Consecutive reelection to the legislature had been common practice in Mexico for most of the nineteenth century and until 1933. The previous experiment with nonconsecutive reelection dates back to the 1814 *Carta de Apatzingan*, whose Article 57 stated that deputies could be reelected after an intervening full term. However, subsequent constitutions lifted that ban, making reelection possible and not setting term limits. The Constitutions of 1824,

1843, 1847, 1857, and 1917 did not mention any prohibition of unlimited consecutive reelection for legislators. By the time the 1933 constitutional reform prohibiting consecutive reelection was enacted, more than 100 years had passed during which legislators at all levels and throughout the country had built their careers through the institution of reelection (see Béjar, "La Reelección parlamentaria en México," pp. 29–33).

In the case of the presidency, reelection had been allowed in various forms since the adoption of the 1824 Constitution. On November 27, 1911, then president Francisco I. Madero enacted a reform that banned presidential reelection, and the clause was left unaltered in the 1917 Constitution. Indeed, the nonreelection clause for the Office of the President was Madero's principal demand during the early days of the Mexican revolution. The situation changed with a reform that was enacted in 1927, which once again canceled the prohibition and allowed reelection, but only after one term had elapsed. For a detailed account, see Careaga, "Reformas institucionales que fracasan," pp. 32–33; see also Manuel González Oropeza, "Comentario al Artículo 83," in Cámara de Diputados, *Derechos del pueblo mexicano,* vol. 9, pp. 335–42.

[5] For a detailed description of the process, see Manuel Barquín Alvarez, "Comentario al Artículo 59," in Cámara de Diputados, ibid., pp. 271–84.

[6] Nacif-Hernández, "The Mexican Chamber of Deputies," p. 52.

[7] See Alberto Arnaut, "El Partido Nacional Revolucionario y la no-reelección consecutiva de legisladores" (paper presented at a meeting entitled La No-Reelección Consecutiva de los Legisladores y el Sistema Político Mexicano, sponsored by Centro de Investigación y Docencia Económicas, Mexico City, March 11, 1996).

[8] Ibid.; see also Marván, *Y Después del presidencialismo?*

[9] Weldon, untitled manuscript, 1994, pp. 16 and 13.

[10] Nacif-Hernández, "The Mexican Chamber of Deputies," pp. 52–54.

[11] For a detailed account of the 1964 attempt to reinstall consecutive reelection, see Careaga, "Reformas institucionales que fracasan"; also see Maite Careaga, "El Fracaso de la reforma reeleccionista de 1964" (manuscript, n.d.). For a broader perspective, see Adolfo Christlieb Ibarrola, *Crónicas de la no-reelección* (Mexico City: Ediciones de Acción Nacional, 1965); and Carlos Madrazo, *La Tesis contra la reelección immediata de los diputados y senadores del Congreso de la Unión* (Mexico City: Partido Revolucionario Institucional, 1965).

[12] For a similar argument on the weakening effects of the nonreelectionist clause on the Mexican Congress, see Marván, *Y Después del presidencialismo?* pp. 92–97.

¹³ See Campos, "Un Congreso sin congresistas." Many incoming deputies may have had other types of experience—as local deputies or senators, for example—but not Chamber experience. A similar situation is evident in Costa Rica, another nonreelectionist country, where, between 1949 and 1998, only 13 percent of its Assembly members were reelected only once; the remaining 87 percent served only one term (see Scott Mainwaring and Matthew Soberg Shugart, eds., *Presidentialism and Democracy in Latin America* [Cambridge and New York: Cambridge University Press, 1997], p. 207).

¹⁴ Gregorio Velázquez served in the 39th, 41st, and 43rd Legislatures.

¹⁵ See Benito Nacif-Hernández "La No Reelección legislativa," *Diálogo y Debate de Cultura Politica* 1, July–September 1997, pp. 160–61.

¹⁶ This topic is explored in detail in chapter 6 of this book.

¹⁷ A similar pattern can be observed in other countries in which bureaucratic careers tend to be highly rewarded in political terms, causing the central government to enjoy higher prestige and to attract more competent public servants, at least at the highest levels. France, India, Japan, and many Latin American countries, among others, are in that group.

¹⁸ Both terms come from Schelinger's theory of political ambition and are used by Benito Nacif-Hernández in a similar argument to analyze ambitions and opportunities for members of the Mexican Chamber of Deputies (see Nacif-Hernández, "The Mexican Chamber of Deputies," pp. 101–36).

¹⁹ According to Gabbert, "Congress serves as a step in the career ladder of the upwardly mobile PRI politician and a sinecure to reward the party faithful. The Mexican system of no re-election doctrine…produces a 'circulation of elites.' In this game of musical chairs, the Chamber of Deputies, far more than the Senate, serves as a training and testing ground for the ambitious young men and women of the PRI" (see Jack B. Gabbert, "The Mexican Chief Executive," in *Chief Executives: National Political Leadership in the United States, Mexico, Great Britain, Germany and Japan*, ed. Taketsugu Tsurutani and Jack B. Gabbert [Spokane: Washington State University Press, 1992], pp. 82–83).

Costa Rica is similar to Mexico in that its legislators can serve a subsequent term only after sitting out at least one full term. There too "politicians cannot expect Assembly careers…. Thus, Costa Rican legislators aspiring to build political careers need to look elsewhere besides the Assembly." Frequently, outgoing legislators try to be appointed to positions in the administration, and this has become the most attractive route for consolidating a political career. Since the president of the republic commands a vast array of resources and influence for boosting politicians' careers, the presidency becomes the focal point for lobbying efforts on the part of ambitious legislators (see John M. Carey, "Strong Candidates for a Limited Office: Presidentialism and Political Parties in

Costa Rica," in Mainwaring and Shugart, eds., *Presidentialism and Democracy in Latin America*, p. 207).

[20] Again, I am using Schelinger's concept as used in Nacif-Hernández's 1995 study (see Nacif-Hernández, "The Mexican Chamber of Deputies," p. 107). Also see how the concept is used by Pipa Norris in *Passages to Power: Legislative Recruitment in Advanced Democracies* (Cambridge and New York: Cambridge University Press, 1997).

[21] The offices included in the figure are the most relevant and visible political offices in Mexico. The construction of the figure was based on personal interviews and on analyses of deputies' political careers between 1970 and 1997 (see *Diccionario biográfico del gobierno mexicano*, 1984, 1987, 1989, and 1992; also see Nacif-Hernández, "The Mexican Chamber of Deputies," p. 109).

[22] Even if most outgoing deputies sought higher office relentlessly, not all of them succeeded. Some may have done so immediately, others may have had to wait for some time, and still others may have never consolidated a political career. But the relevant fact is that most made the attempt and, in doing so, generated a pattern of behavior that will be analyzed in detail in chapter 5 of this book.

[23] Nacif-Hernández's study supports this argument: "non-continuous re-election … encourages other strategies of career advancement which mainly focus on two office opportunities—Senate seats and state governorships. Promotion from the Chamber to the Senate is a usual pattern of advancement that raises expectations among many PRI Deputies. State governorships are more distant office goals, but the Chamber of Deputies clearly appears as a relevant office experience in political careers leading to the office of governor" (see Nacif-Hernández, "The Mexican Chamber of Deputies," p. 139).

[24] These low figures reflect the growing tendency to recruit *técnicos* rather than *políticos* into high-ranking positions in the executive branch. In general, political and electoral experience does not seem to be valued by the administration. According to Cornelius, "[m]ore than one-third of the national bureaucratic elite in 1984 held master's degrees, and both the de la Madrid and Salinas administrations had ample representation of people at the cabinet and sub-cabinet level who had earned doctorates at elite U.S. and European universities" (see Wayne A. Cornelius and Ann L. Craig, *The Mexican Political System in Transition* [San Diego: Center for U.S.-Mexican Studies, University of California at San Diego, 1991], p. 46). For a discussion of recruiting patterns in Mexico, especially the role of technocrats within the administration, see Miguel Angel Centeno, *Democracy Within Reason: Technocratic Revolution in Mexico* (Philadelphia: Pennsylvania State University Press, 1994); Rogelio Hernández, "La División de la elite política mexicana," in *Lecturas 73 del trimestre económico: México: Auge, crisis y ajuste I*, ed. Carlos Bazdrech et al. (Mexico

City: Fondo de Cultura Económica, 1992); Gilberto Ramírez and E. Salim, *La Clase política mexicana* (Mexico City: EDAMEX, 1987); and Francisco Suárez Farías, *Elite, tecnocracia y movilidad política en México* (Mexico City: Universidad Autónoma Metropolitana, Xochimilco, 1991).

[25]See Nacif-Hernández,"The Mexican Chamber of Deputies," p. 128, table 3.8.

[26] Ibid., p. 126.

[27] Here I assume that progressive ambition dominates career strategies and is the reason for dismissing state assembly seats as an option. On the other hand, beyond Senate seats and governorships, only one more elected office remains—the presidency of the republic. Deputies perceive this office as too distant and unfeasible to be considered as a goal for their next elected office.

[28] One way to reduce the fears may be through the introduction of term limits, which can preclude some of the patronage practices observed in other countries.

[29] The last initiative to permit consecutive reelection, presented on October 29, 1998, proposed allowing one reelection for senators and three for deputies; after these terms in office, legislators can run again for the same office if one term intervenes (see the Web site of the Chamber of Deputies at <http://gaceta.cddhcu.gob.mx/Gaceta/1998/oct/981028.html>). Over the last several years, other initiatives have been presented. According to Weldon, "there was talk of permitting the re-election of deputies and senators in the fall of 1991, but the proposals were quickly torpedoed. Again in the fall of 1994, there were renewed proposals to reinstitute congressional re-election. The issue [was] brought up frequently in the 1995–96 interparty negotiations over the electoral reform" (see Weldon, "Political Sources of *Presidencialismo* in Mexico," p. 256).

[30] See *Querétaro*, January 23, 2000.

CHAPTER FIVE

PARTISAN POWERS OF THE PRESIDENT

THE MEXICAN PRESIDENT TRADITIONALLY HAD A CRUCIAL ROLE TO play in determining the political future of legislators who belonged to the Institutional Revolutionary Party. To do so there were two sets of powers at the president's disposal, the combined effect of which gave the president considerable influence over the advancement of PRI deputies' careers. On the one hand, the Constitution granted legal powers to the chief executive to appoint federal government officials. On the other hand, "metaconstitutional"—or partisan—powers enabled the Mexican president to appoint PRI candidates to various elected posts. In order to thoroughly understand the influence of the presidential institution on legislative behavior during the last decades, it is necessary to analyze both sets of powers. In fact, presidential partisan powers were the key to explaining why Mexican presidents displayed in practice greater powers than those conferred upon them by the Constitution.[1]

After a non-PRI president takes office in December 2000, it will be interesting to analyze the evolution of the presidential institution that comes as a result of this change. On the one hand, formal and constitutional powers will remain intact, unless constitutional reforms are passed to expand or limit presidential powers. On the other hand, the president's informal and partisan powers will probably suffer the most, because Vicente Fox will probably not wield the kind of leverage that his PRI predecessors were able to exert over their party. Consequently, Fox will have fewer resources with which to reward allies and punish adversaries, and therefore he will command a lower level of discipline and control over the leadership of his party, the National Action Party. In fact, Felipe Calderón, the newly elected leader of the PAN delegation to Congress, has stated that the PAN parliamentary group intends to display autonomy and independence when dealing with the chief executive. Luis Felipe Bravo Mena, president of the PAN National Committee, reiterated Calderón's statement, when he said that his party will maintain a respectful but independent relationship with the new president. As partisan powers get detached from the presidential office, the nature and logic of presidential politics will undoubtedly undergo a dramatic transformation.

THE PRESIDENTIAL INSTITUTION IN MEXICO

The president is the most important figure in Mexican politics, and the presidency is the most resourceful organization in the political system. By occupying the office, regardless of personal qualifications, the Mexican president commands a wide array of political, economic, intelligence, and military resources. Even as Vicente Fox's presidency is expected to display less control over political actors, the president will continue to be the most influential player in Mexican politics.

Over the last decades, many scholars have studied the Mexican presidency and they tend to agree that the presidency is the pivotal office of political power in the country. Gabbert noted that "the presidency is the keystone in the governmental and political structure of the Mexican republic ... the decision-making center of the Mexican political system."[2] For Crespo, the presidential institution is the "central column of the [Mexican] regime ... the point of convergence ... the arbiter of the conflicts among political and social groups."[3] In 1972, Cosío Villegas wrote that the two most important institutions in the Mexican political system are the presidential institution and the country's official party, the PRI.[4] According to Sánchez Susarrey, the main instruments of negotiation and representation in Mexican politics are the presidential institution and the corporatist organizations (most of which are affiliated with the PRI).[5] Finally, Arnaldo Córdova considered Mexico's president the "supreme arbiter" to whom major political actors appealed to gain legitimacy and to resolve differences.[6]

Given the centrality and preeminence of the office during the twentieth century, it became a truism to say that Mexican presidents were all-powerful actors with no restraints on their will, reflecting a reality and also creating a myth of the dictatorial-like presidency, to borrow the term used by novelist Vargas Llosa some years ago. Because of the common perception that the Mexican presidency concentrated greater power than desirable, various terms reflecting "excessiveness" were applied to describe the nature of Mexico's system. These terms included "hyperpresidential,"[7] "highly presidential,"[8] "authoritarian presidency,"[9] "absolute sexennial monarchy,"[10] and "omnipotent presidency."[11]

Nevertheless, from a strictly constitutional perspective, Mexico has always been classified as having a presidential system with average powers—neither too excessive nor too limited.[12] According to Shugart and Carey's ranking, countries like Korea, Chile, Paraguay, and Brazil, for example, exhibit higher levels of formal presidential powers than Mexico.[13] Furthermore, formal presidential authority has diminished over the last two decades, while congressional powers have expanded.[14] However, it is misleading to focus solely on analyses of formal and constitutional powers because, until now, partisan powers had been a major source of presidential power in Mexico. Informal or metaconstitutional presidential powers explain why Mexican executives were able to govern with considerable access to political resources and with few checks and balances. There is almost universal agreement that the dual role played by the chief executive as head of both the PRI and the executive branch was the key element in explaining metaconstitutional powers and therefore the peculiar "strength" found in the Mexican presidency.[15] Nonetheless, the metaconstitutional dimension has also been reduced in recent years and will certainly be severely curtailed after a non-PRI president takes office in December 2000.

In order to evaluate both the constitutional and the partisan aspects of presidential power in Mexico, an "institutionalist" definition can be proposed. According to this definition, the Mexican presidential institution consists of a set of formal and informal powers that guide and set norms for the president's behavior, constrain his or her actions, and shape the behavior and expectations of other political actors in Mexico.[16] Formal powers are established in the Constitution and make the president the head of state as well as the head of government. Metaconstitutional powers are, on the other hand, informal rules that are not contained in any law. Their roots are in tradition and the nature of the political system, and, even though they are *unwritten laws,* all political players know them and abide by them.[17] It is these metaconstitutional powers that made the president the head of the PRI party during the period covered by this study.

CONSTITUTIONAL POWERS

Article 89 of the Constitution is the main source that defines the formal powers of the president. Until 1994, the most important powers were the following:[18]

1. To appoint and remove freely (that is, without congressional approval) ministers of state, the attorney general, the attorney of the Federal District, the mayor of Mexico City, and all other government employees whose appointment or removal is not otherwise provided for in the Constitution or by law;

2. With the approval of the Senate, to appoint justices, consuls, ambassadors, military officers, high-level employees of the Treasury Ministry, and justices of both the Supreme Court and the Tribunal of the Federal District;

3. To appoint senior managers and directors of most public agencies and state-owned enterprises;[19]

4. To promulgate and enforce laws enacted by Congress (the president has line-item veto powers);

5. To submit proposed laws directly to Congress;

6. To maintain and preserve the internal and the international security of the state through the use of the armed forces and the National Guard and, with congressional approval, to declare war;

7. To conduct monetary policy and decide on issues of domestic and foreign investment;

8. To propose the revenue law and draft the annual budget bill;

9. To publish the *Plan Nacional de Desarrollo*, which contains the general objectives and strategies that guide government policy on economic and social issues on a six-year basis;

10. With the approval of Congress, to formalize international treaties and diplomatic negotiations;

11. To expropriate private property for reasons of general interest; and

12. To establish and carry out educational and cultural policies through the minister of public education.

PARTISAN POWERS OF THE PRESIDENT

Partisan powers refer to the influence Mexican presidents had both in the selection and control of the PRI's leadership and the party's members in Congress and in decisions on the party's candidates for elected offices. More than two decades ago, Carpizo coined the term "metaconstitutional powers" to designate all the presidential powers not contained in the Constitution or in any other law but exerted in practice.[20] He was referring precisely to partisan powers as defined in this chapter.

Presidential partisan powers emerged in the mid-1930s, when then president Lázaro Cárdenas (1934–40) became the *jefe máximo* of the "revolutionary family," meaning that he was not only the head of government but also the "indisputable leader" of the party. The process of attaining this position was twofold. First, Cárdenas was able to eliminate other sources of leadership outside the presidency that had given rise to *caudillismo*: political instability, civil war, and coups d'état in the years preceding his rise to power. To do so, he built a broad coalition and expelled Plutarco Elías Calles from the country. Calles had founded the National Revolutionary Party (forerunner of the PRI) in 1929 and served as the party's de facto leader for many years.[21] Second, Cárdenas changed the structure and the name of the original PNR to Mexican Revolutionary Party (*Partido de la Revolución Mexicana*, PRM) in 1938. He reorganized the party along sectoral lines—workers, peasants, and the military—and, by doing so, became the uncontested leader not only of the party but also of the entire "revolutionary family." This corporatist structure allowed successive presidents and leaders of the PRM—and later of the PRI (starting in 1946)—to control party members and reward them via allocation of elected offices based on a quota system, which prevailed strongly until the late 1980s.

It was during the Cárdenas presidency that the chief executive assumed de facto leadership of the party, and with it the informal power to handpick PRI candidates for elected offices; the presidency became institutionalized as well. By expelling *caudillo* Elías Calles in 1935, Cárdenas made the office of the presidency dependent on the institution rather than on the person who occupied it, and he established the foundations of modern Mexican presidentialism.[22] By corporatizing the party structure and making its leader his agent, Cárdenas acquired partisan powers that laid the basis for future Mexican presidents to control PRI policies and decisions, and as a by-product, to curb *caudillismo* and violence. According to Miguel Angel Centeno, "both the PRI and the strong presidency did provide the institutional stability which allowed Mexico to recuperate from the Revolution. The concentration of power on the incumbent, combined with the no-re-election clause, also prevented the consolidation of one-man rule."[23]

Indeed, the Cárdenas period has been described as constituting the second period of the era of presidentialism in Mexico. The first corresponds to the drafting of the 1917 Constitution, in which the formal foundations of the presidency were laid out. The second, corresponding to Cárdenas's term as president (1934–40), set the foundation for the partisan powers of the presidency and made its occupant the indisputable leader of the political elite. The third era translated these powers into actual policy and political decisions—on economic, social, and political issues—making the presidency the most important institution in Mexico's social and political life.[24]

The partisan powers that emerged in the 1930s expanded presidential authority well beyond its constitutional boundaries and contributed to an image of "excessiveness" and lack of accountability.[25] Consequently, presidentialism in Mexico became synonymous with unrestrained and even authoritarian rule. As informal presidential authority diminished (as has been the case in recent years), Mexican presidentialism has become increasingly restricted to its purely legal domain and is destined to become part of a constitutional and democratic form of government. In all probability, this tendency will be consolidated under the presidency of Vicente Fox, because—unlike the PRI presidents who preceded him—he will not have the informal powers and political instruments needed to control his party and its congressional delegations. The following section provides a description and a brief history of the development of the principal partisan powers of PRI presidents.

Leadership of the PRI

Although there has always been an official chair and a formal hierarchy within the party, it was the president who made or approved major decisions and designated the party's leadership.[26] Heading the party was a necessary condition for all remaining metaconstitutional powers. By virtue of being the party's real leader, the president had the power to select its candidates for office as well as its leaders in Congress.

Selection of Candidates

One of the immediate consequences of nonreelection was the president's personal involvement in the selection of PRI candidates for governorships, the Senate, key positions in Congress, and some mayoralties, in addition to his or her own successor. Nonreelectability created a system of mandatory office rotation at federal, state, and municipal levels—a situation that limited the voters' role in rewarding incumbents and increased the influence of the party and the president in the selection of candidates. Indeed, Cárdenas was the first beneficiary of the nonreelection clause, when in 1934, still as a presidential candidate, he participated in drafting lists of candidates for Congress.[27] This informal practice not only continued after Cárdenas left office but also was reinforced as time went by; it became one of the primary informal institutions governing the behavior of PRI-affiliated politicians in Mexico.

Until very recently, the president had full control over the selection of PRI candidates for all elected offices. The most important example was the use of so-called *dedazo* (handpicking) in determining presidential succession. This process operated via *el destape* (unveiling of the candidate), by which the president concealed his or her preferred candidate (*el tapado*) until the proper time and then simply communicated the choice to party leaders. Then, the *tapado* was *destapado*, that is, the candidate was unveiled and nominated. These terms denote a highly vertical and closed process, yet one that enjoyed legitimacy and effectiveness until the early 1980s. According to Cornelius and Craig, "state governors ... the leaders of Congress and the PRI, some high-ranking military officers, the heads of state-owned industrial enterprises, and hundreds of other officeholders [were] handpicked by each incoming president."[28] In his book, Carpizo wrote that "the president [had] the final say in choosing governors," and as an example, quoted Braulio Maldonado, former governor of Baja California, who told the following story about his own selection process and that of other leaders: "I was chosen ... by the president of the republic ... and all officeholders of our country, high- or low-ranking, have been chosen in the same way, from 1928 to the present. This is an axiomatic truth."[29]

During his term in office, President Zedillo (1994–2000) limited his interference in these selection processes. Over the last few years, as the PRI began to hold open primary elections to select candidates, the president's influence decreased accordingly. However, for most of the period under study, the president had the final word in decisions about candidacies after negotiations among party leaders and other political actors had taken place. Former president López Portillo (1976–82) coined the phrase that presidents are "*el fiel de la balanza,*" meaning that he allowed everyone to express opinions, but that he made the final decision.[30]

Selection of Congressional Party Leadership

The president chose the majority leaders of both the Chamber of Deputies and the Senate—which obviously required a PRI majority in both houses.[31] In doing so, he was exerting control over legislators directly and indirectly through the congressional speaker, who was an agent of the chief executive.[32]

The electoral predominance of the PRI over the period of study—from the executive branch to the legislative branch and across most of the state and local governments—played a major role in preserving these metaconstituional powers. When the PRI had control over most political offices in Mexico, any ambitious politician knew that the PRI was the only route to power, and therefore, there was only one set of rules to follow in order to be "successful." The more predominant the PRI was electorally, the stronger the president's leadership and control were over the political class. As political competition has grown, and other parties have become effective routes to political power—to the extent that a member of the National Action Party will now head the presidency—ambitious politicians have begun to evaluate the costs and benefits of opting for PRI affiliation. Because PRI candidacies can no longer guarantee electoral success, their appeal as an instrument of reward has diminished considerably, as has the influence of the president. It is therefore obvious that the PRI's successful track record in winning elections during the period of this study facilitated the functioning of the presidential system of political nomination and reward.

REVERSED ACCOUNTABILITY

Studies of the U.S. Congress regard reelection as the most powerful incentive for legislators to consider themselves accountable to the electorate. Mayhew wrote that the desire to be reelected establishes an "electoral connection" between politicians and voters: politicians provide services to their constituents in order to increase their chances of staying in office; voters determine whether politicians should be rewarded by means of reelection.[33] In the Mexican case, however, the nonreelection clause has diluted this electoral connection and therefore reduced the degree of political accountability legislators felt toward their constituencies.[34] A process that stimulated legislators' responsiveness to the executive branch and the party ran both parallel and counter to the process of political disengagement taking place between legislators and voters. This close rapport between Mexican legislators and the executive branch was a consequence of the president's ability to promote and reward loyal deputies with office candidacies as well as appointments to positions in the administration.[35]

In past decades, Mexican presidents exercised their power to advance PRI legislators' political careers in two important ways: on the one hand, they used their constitutional and formal authority to appoint individuals to administrative offices; on the other hand, they took advantage of their informal power to influence the nomination of PRI candidates to all elected posts. Therefore, PRI deputies had few incentives to serve their constituents but many reasons to seek political patronage from the president. In practice, the president was able to reward deputies with offices in the bureaucracy or with PRI candidacies to elected office. Consequently, the direction of political accountability was inverted—it was taken away from the voters, who mattered little because they could not reward their representatives, and given to the chief executive, who could promote political careers in Mexico.

According to the new "institutionalist" approach, institutions are the rules of the game that shape the behavior and interactions of individuals and organizations: they can determine and constrain behavior by rewarding and sanctioning alternative courses of action. In doing so, institutions establish a range of possible options, creating certain patterns of stable and predictable behavior. In trying to anticipate the payoffs for different courses of action, given a set of formal and informal institutions, individuals behave in a way that will maximize the expected reward.[36] In Mexico, PRI deputies were faced with several institutions that directly shaped, determined, and restricted their behavior in terms of possible strategies for advancing

Table 5.1
**Principal Institutions Faced by Deputies
in Terms of Career Advancement**

Institution	Type	Direct Consequence of Incentives Created
Nonconsecutive reelection	Formal (Constitution, Article 59), stable, and predictable.	Impossibility to run for same office. Deputies seek opportunities elsewhere.
President's power to decide major PRI candidacies	Informal, nonwritten, widely known, and established by tradition.	Need to lobby and appeal to the president in order to be electable.
President's power to appoint government officials	Formal, written (Constitution, Article 89).	Need to lobby and appeal to the president in order to be electable.

their political careers. These are outlined in table 5.1, along with the consequences they produced.

The dominant strategic behavior that arose from these institutions was that PRI deputies, aspiring to higher office (mainly Senate seats and governorships), had to lobby and appeal to the principal nominator—that is, the president of the republic in his role as party chief—and to those who could influence the president (such as party leaders, cabinet members, special interest groups, and the media). By controlling nominations to major offices, the president became the focal point of efforts of ambitious deputies eager to advance their careers, who then became accountable to the chief executive rather than to the electorate. This phenomenon, called reversed accountability, completely changed the direction of political accountability—from below (the electorate) to above (the presidency).[37]

The reversed-accountability hypothesis is supported by empirical evidence. Personal interviews were conducted with members of the three major parties, in which they were asked about their perceptions of

Table 5.2
Likely Motivations of PRI Deputies
(opinions by party group)[a]
(1 = least important, 5 = most important)
(N = 49)

Motivation	Party			Weighted Average
	PRI	PAN	PRD	
To support the president of the republic	4.4	5.0	4.6	**4.5**
To follow the Speaker's mandate and goals	4.3	4.9	4.0	**4.4**
To protect the administration from opposition criticisms	4.3	4.8	4.2	**4.3**
To advance one's own political career	3.8	4.9	4.7	**4.2**
To follow the party's mandate and program	3.9	4.9	3.4	**4.0**
To carry out personal ideals and commitments	3.8	3.2	2.1	**3.3**
To fulfill voters' demands	2.7	1.4	1.7	**2.1**
To oversee and control the executive branch	2.4	1.1	1.5	**1.8**

Note: Shading indicates highest grades by party.
[a] Question asked of deputies: In your opinion, how important is each of the following motives in explaining the behavior of PRI deputies, on a scale 1–5, where 1 means that the motive is not important, and 5 means that the motive is very important?
Source: Personal interviews.

PRI deputies' behavior. The weighted scores of their responses are shown in table 5.2. The following conclusions can be drawn from their responses:

1. The main motivation behind PRI deputies' actions was considered to be responding to the mandate of someone from above. Deputies saw PRI members' main priorities as supporting the president of the republic, following the Speaker's mandate, and protecting the administration from the opposition's criticisms.

2. In contrast, being accountable to constituencies was judged to be a somewhat irrelevant motivation for PRI deputies: the fulfillment of voters' demands appeared as the second *least* important motivation for PRI deputies, a perception with which even the *priístas* themselves agreed.

3. Deputies from all the major parties regarded oversight of the executive branch as the *least* important of the motivations behind PRI deputies' actions. This result is quite remarkable because the legislators' opinions contradict the system of checks and balances that has been established in the Mexican Constitution, and they ignore the electorate's mandate that members of Congress assume a more active role in exercising control over the government.[38]

Given PRI deputies' incentives to advance their political careers and the strategic behavior that accompanied this aim, legislative oversight of the government was not considered a valuable instrument for election to higher office (as the scores in table 5.2 show). On the contrary, controlling and overseeing the executive branch—that is, the office of the nominator or principal—ran counter to political rationale. If the primary strategy for a PRI deputy's political advancement was to lobby the chief executive, then overseeing the administration's activities could have harmed the chances of being considered for future office. This pattern of behavior translated into concrete parliamentary practices that weakened the Mexican Congress, including (1) voting in order to please the chief executive, (2) avoiding actions that harmed the administration, (3) abdicating legislative authority to the executive branch, and (4) ignoring cases of mismanagement.[39]

Information derived from the deputies' responses to interview questions on this topic supports this argument: the principal factors impeding legislative oversight are motivational or behavioral in nature—that is, accountability is reversed—as well as the inexperience and limited professionalism of legislators, which is a direct result of their inability to be reelected to consecutive terms. The weighted scores of respondents' opinions are presented in table 5.3.

Table 5.3
Factors Obstructing Legislative Oversight, 1994–97
(as perceived by deputies)
(1 = most obstructive, 5 = least obstructive)
(N = 49)

Factor	Grade	Type of Factor
Systematic attitude of PRI deputies to protect and safeguard the executive branch	3.80	Motivational
Political influence and control exerted by the president over the PRI congressional group	3.62	Motivational
Lack of parliamentary experience of most deputies (due to the nonreelection clause)	3.59	Capability
PRI occupation of Supervisory Committee's chair every year until 1994	3.51	Motivational
Lack of deputies' technical expertise in financial matters and activities related to oversight	3.46	Capability
Lack of application or enforcement of the legal authority that exists but is insufficient	3.38	Motivational

Source: Personal interviews and table 5.2.

THE RECENT TRANSFORMATION IN THE PRESIDENT'S APPOINTMENT AND PARTISAN POWERS

The presidential institution has undergone dramatic changes over the past few years, to the extent that the nature of the Mexican presidential system has been altered forever. Even before the election of a non-PRI candidate to the presidency in July 2000, the supposedly "omnipotent" powers of the president had already diminished to a considerable degree.

Alicia Hernández Chavez labeled the years 1917–40 "the empowerment period" of the presidency and the 1960s "the climax period," when a large public sector provided ample resources for presidential control and patronage. According to Hernández, since the early

1980s, presidential power has been gradually limited as a result of the various reforms that have been implemented from within the government (for example, electoral reforms and federalism). She defined this historical process as the "parabola of Mexican presidentialism."[40] Aguilar Villanueva maintained that the Mexican process of democratic transition since the early 1980s was accompanied by a voluntary and gradually self-limiting process, in which the presidency itself retrenched from various activities in the economic and political arena.[41] Jesús Orozco Henríquez wrote that, from the 1920s to the 1960s, presidential powers tended to increase in an effort to strengthen the president's role in guiding the building of the state. Starting in the 1970s, the process began to slowly reverse its course, strengthening the legislative and the judicial branches of government.[42] Finally, Lujambio pointed out that "since 1988 the Mexican president has experienced a progressive weakening of his powers," both in their constitutional and partisan spheres. As examples, Lujambio cited (1) the autonomy that has been granted to the Federal Electoral Institute since 1996, (2) the creation of autonomous agrarian tribunals in 1992, (3) the election of the mayor of Mexico City beginning in 1997, (4) the increased autonomy of the Central Bank since 1993, (5) the lengthening of congressional sessions, and (6) the right granted to the Senate in 1994 to confirm the president's nominee for attorney general.[43]

However, beyond the formal constitutional limitations on presidential powers, the most important factor restricting the president's informal powers may be the limits Vicente Fox and his successors will likely face in their attempts to lead and control Congress and their parties. This change should help to bring about a more balanced and mutually independent relationship between the executive branch on the one hand, and Congress, state governments, and other elected officials on the other. Since 1997, President Zedillo had begun to face unprecedented autonomy and even conflict on the part of Congress members, but he maintained a tight grip on the PRI delegation to the Chamber of Deputies and the party's majority in the Senate, which provided a safety valve for him. When Fox assumes power, he will face a Congress in which his party will not command a majority in either house, and he himself may not have political leadership over some important sectors of his own party.

Appointment Powers

Over the past several years, various legal changes have limited the president's appointment powers. Some of the major changes include the following:

1. The most relevant change is that the chief of the Federal District (the mayor of Mexico City) and the heads of the 16 city councils (*delegaciones*) are no longer appointed by the president but elected by popular vote. This is a change of major proportions in presidential powers because of the Mexico City government's capabilities and financial resources—the city has 8.5 million inhabitants, its budget is equivalent to 5.1 percent of federal outlays, and its production constitutes 24 percent of the country's gross national product.[44]

2. As of 1994, the appointment of the attorney general requires Senate confirmation, but the president is still responsible for nominating candidates.

3. Prior to 1994, Supreme Court justices were appointed by the chief executive, subject to Senate confirmation. Now the president merely submits a list of candidates from which the Senate selects the justices.

Partisan Powers

During President Zedillo's administration, many changes were made within the sphere of his metaconstitutional powers to select candidates for office and party officials. The reforms and some of their results are described in the following paragraphs.

One of President Zedillo's major contributions to Mexico's democracy was undoubtedly his consent to a change in the rules governing the selection of PRI candidates for elected offices. Although no set of stable and clear rules was passed, in 1997 a tendency arose—based on trial and error—to select candidates through primaries. As early as November 1994, then president-elect Zedillo had proposed to establish a "healthy distance" (*sana distancia*) between the party and the presidency. Although his proposal was not reflected in the way party leaders continued to be selected, the idea of holding primaries to select PRI candidates began to gain momentum after 1997. The first open and regulated exercise in primary elections occurred successfully in 1998, in the State of Chihuahua in northern Mexico, when a variety of PRI candidates openly campaigned across the state. In the end, a local politician, with no direct ties either to the center or to the president, was nominated to and subsequently won the governorship.[45] After that experiment, other states began to undergo similar selection processes.

The most relevant case in point, however, was the primary election held in November 1999 to select the PRI's presidential candidate. Four candidates had campaigned across the country, and in spite of accusations that the PRI's "official candidate" was Francisco Labastida, the process established a benchmark for future electoral experiments. Given Mexican presidents' previous influence over the political elite—derived from their powers to handpick the party's presidential candidates—holding a PRI primary in 1999 established a major transformation in the logic of presidential politics in Mexico, even before the PRI's defeat at the polls in July 2000.

Nevertheless, other candidacies continued to be decided behind the scenes. President Zedillo may have indeed retrenched from direct participation, but PRI governors and party officials still wielded a great deal of leverage in the selection of candidates. The selection of candidates for the 2000 election to the Senate and the Chamber of Deputies, for example, produced disenchantment and discord among many PRI members, because the process was perceived as just another round of "clientelism" and patronage by which to reward allies and party bosses.

The most significant change in presidential partisan powers is still to come, however, because the next president of Mexico, Vicente Fox, will undoubtedly have fewer political resources at his disposal—at least in comparison with past presidents—to use for commanding discipline and loyalty from members of Congress and his own party. Even if a PRI president were to win a presidential election in the future, the ability to exert the same influence and control over the party would be lost. As the PRI becomes an opposition party, the logic that guides its relationship with the executive branch will change forever.

In summary, the president's formal and informal powers to promote political careers—and the resources needed to implement these powers effectively—have decreased dramatically over the last decade. These limitations on the president's ability to help advance legislators' political careers had already begun to affect PRI deputies' discipline and behavior, even prior to the party's electoral defeat in July 2000. The results of that election have only altered PRI legislators' sense of discipline and loyalty. The following chapter will explain the transformation in detail.

Notes

[1] See Manuel Camacho Solís, "Los Nudos históricos del sistema político mexicano," in *Las Crisis en el sistema político mexicano, 1928–1977* (Mexico City: Colegio de México, 1977); Gabbert, "The Mexican Chief Executive"; and Alonso Lujambio, "Adios a la excepcionalidad: Régimen presidencial y gobierno dividido en México," *Este País* 10 (February 2000). Mainwaring and Shugart noted that "Mexican presidents derive their apparent dominance not from the presidential constitution, but from their overwhelming partisan powers" (see Mainwaring and Shugart, eds., *Presidentialism and Democracy in Latin America*, p. 8). According to Casar, the hegemonic party system is the source of hyperpresidentialism (see María Amparo Casar, "Las Bases político-institucionales del poder presidencial en México," *Política y Gobierno* 1, no. 1 [1996]). For Reyes Heroles, the problem with Mexican presidentialism is not the written norm but the symbiosis between the chief executive and state governors, aided by an electoral rule that helped a hegemonic system prevail for many decades (see Federico Reyes Heroles, "Porqué del presidencialismo," *Diálogo y Debate de Cultura Política*, July–September 1997).

[2] Gabbert "The Mexican Chief Executive," p. 61.

[3] José Antonio Crespo, *Jaque al rey: Hacia un nuevo presidencialimo en México* (Mexico City: Editorial Joaquín Mortiz, 1996), p. 12.

[4] See Daniel Cosío Villegas, *El Sistema político mexicano* (Mexico City: Editorial Joaquín Mortiz, 1972).

[5] See Jaime Sánchez Susarrey, *La Transición incierta* (Mexico City: Editorial Vuelta, 1991).

[6] See Arnaldo Córdova, *La Formación del poder político en México* (Mexico City: Ediciones Era, 1993 [1972]).

[7] See Casar, "Las Bases político-institucionales."

[8] See George Philip, *The Presidency in Mexican Politics* (New York: St. Martin's Press, 1992).

[9] See Kenneth F. Johnson, "Mexico's Authoritarian Presidency," in *Presidential Power in Latin American Politics*, ed. Thomas V. DeBacco (New York: Praeger Publishers, 1977).

[10] See Cosío Villegas, *El Sistema presidencial en México*.

[11] Frank Ralph Brandenburg, *The Making of Modern Mexico* (Englewood Cliffs, N.J.: Prentice-Hall, 1964). For Weldon, there were four necessary conditions for *presidencialismo* in Mexico to exist (he was referring not to the system of government—that is, Sartori's definition—but to the "excessive" type of presidency): (1) a presidentialist system based on the Constitution; (2) unified government, where the ruling party controls the presidency and both houses of Congress; (3) discipline within the ruling party; and (4) a president who is the acknowledged leader of the ruling party. If any of these four conditions ceased to exist, the equilibrium of *presidencialismo* would begin to break down (see Weldon, "Political Sources of *Presidencialismo* in Mexico," p. 227) .

[12] See Casar, "Las Bases político-institucionales"; and Reyes Heroles, "Porqué del presidencialismo."

[13] Matthew Soberg Shugart and John M. Carey, *Presidents and Assemblies: Constitutional Design and Electoral Dynamics* (Cambridge and New York: Cambridge University Press, 1992), pp. 154–57.

[14] See María Amparo Casar, "Las Relaciones entre el Poder Ejecutivo y el Legislativo: El Caso de México," *Política y Gobierno* 6, no. 1 (1999); Jesús Orozco Henríquez,"El Sistema presidencial en el constituyente de Querétaro y su evolución posterior," in *El Sistema presidencial mexicano* (Mexico City: Instituto de Investigaciones Jurídicas, Universidad Nacional Autónoma de México, 1988); and Lujambio, "Adios a la excepcionalidad." As a system of government, presidentialism does not necessarily imply authoritarian forms of political control. On the contrary, most of the presidential regimes in the world, including those in the Americas (the United States included), are currently democratic. According to Sartori, the characteristics of a presidential system are the following: (1) the president is elected by popular vote, (2) the president cannot be removed by a parliamentary vote during the term in office, and (3) the president is the head of government and appoints its members (see Giovanni Sartori, *Comparative Constitutional Engineering: An Inquiry into*

Structures, Incentives, and Outcomes [New York: New York University Press, 1994], pp. 83–86). For a review of different definitions of presidential systems, see Shugart and Carey, *Presidents and Assemblies*, pp. 18–22.

[15] See Casar, "Las Bases político-institucionales"; Camacho Solís, "Los Nudos históricos del sistema político mexicano"; Gabbert, "The Mexican Chief Executive"; and Reyes Heroles "Porqué del Presidencialismo." Also see note 1 in this chapter.

[16] Here I follow Keohane's definition of institutions as "persistent and connected sets of rules (formal and informal) which prescribe behavioral roles, constrain activity, and shape expectations" (see Robert Keohane, "Neoliberal Institutionalism: A Perspective on World Politics," in *International Institutions and State Power* [Boulder, Colo.: Westview Press, 1989], p. 3). North presented a similar definition (see North, *Institutions, Institutional Change, and Economic Performance*). In the Mexican literature, Roberto Blum used an institutionalist definition: presidentialism as the set of formal and informal powers at the disposal of the president of the republic (see Roberto Blum Valenzuela , *De la Política mexicana y sus medios* [Mexico City: Editorial Miguel Angel Porrúa and Centro de Investigación para el Desarrollo, A.C.,1996]).

[17] Twenty years ago, Carpizo used legal terms to analyze and distinguish the sources of presidential power in Mexico, one being the Constitution and the rule of law, and the other being tradition and conventions (see Carpizo, *El Presidencialismo mexicano*).

[18] Some of those powers have changed since 1994. Perhaps the most relevant one is that the chief of Mexico City's government is no longer a presidential appointee but an elected official who emerges from an open and contested election (see current Article 89, which is posted on the following Web site: <http://info4.juridicas.unam.mx/unijus/fed/12/90.htm>).

[19] The size of the so-called *sector paraestatal* has varied over time. Today, there are about 230 state-owned enterprises and developmental agencies. However, in the early 1980s, the number was as high as 1,155 (see table 3.1).

[20] Carpizo, *El Presidencialismo mexicano*.

[21] Plutarco Elías Calles was president of the republic from 1924 to 1928. Alvaro Obregón, who was to become his successor in December 1928, was assassinated a few months before his inauguration. In order to curb political violence, end the *caudillista* era, and make the transition to an era of institutions, as he envisioned, Calles founded the PNR in 1929, but he himself also became a *caudillo* by becoming a key political boss of the political class, in addition to being the president. Indeed, the period 1929–36, during which he was the de facto chief of the PNR, is known as *el maximato* because of the political control and influence he exerted at the time. For a detailed discussion of this era, see

Luis Javier Garrido, *El Partido de la Revolución Institucionalizada: La Formación del nuevo estado en México, 1928–1945* (Mexico City: Siglo XXI Editores, 1982).

[22] See Córdova, *La Formación del poder político en México*; and Blum, *De la Política mexicana y sus medios.*

[23] Miguel Angel Centeno, *Democracy Within Reason: Technocratic Revolution in Mexico* (Philadelphia: Pennsylvania State University Press, 1994).

[24] See Casar, "Lås Bases político-institucionales," p. 82.

[25] See Casar, "Las Relaciones entre el Poder Ejecutivo y el Legislativo."

[26] Ample journalistic work on how presidents handpicked PRI leaders has been published. One of the most recent and famous episodes occurred in April 1993, when then president Salinas dismissed PRI chief Genaro Borrego over the telephone. According to newspaper reports, the name of Ortiz Arana, who became Borrego's successor, was transmitted by the same means. More recently, close aides of PRI chief Santiago Oñate (1995–96) have provided evidence about how he was dismissed by President Zedillo in 1997.

[27] See Benito Nacif-Hernández, "La Rotación de cargos legislativos y la evolución del sistema de partidos en México," *Política y Gobierno* 4, no. 1 (1997).

[28] Cornelius and Craig, *The Mexican Political System in Transition*, p. 33.

[29] Carpizo, *El Presidencialismo mexicano,* p. 197.

[30] As is frequently the case with practices that go on behind closed doors, little empirical evidence exists to document this selection process. In his memoirs (*Mis Memorias*), former president López Portillo described several occasions during which he decided on party issues, although he frequently uses metaphorical language to cloud the evidence. Much journalistic work has been produced on this topic. For a description of the informal mechanism of presidential succession in Mexico, or *dedazo*, see Peter Smith, "The 1988 Presidential Succession in Historical Perspective," in *Mexico's Alternative Political Futures*, ed. Wayne A. Cornelius, Judith Gentleman, and Peter H. Smith (San Diego: Center for U.S.-Mexican Studies, University of California at San Diego, 1989); Philip, *The Presidency in Mexican Politics*, pp. 4–6; and Gabbert, "The Mexican Chief Executive," pp. 75–80. For evidence of the role of presidents in handpicking gubernatorial candidates, see Carlos Martínez Assad and Alvaro Arreola, "El poder de los gobernadores," in *La Vida mexicana en la crisis*, ed. Soledad Loaeza and Rafael Segovia (Mexico City: Colegio de México, 1987).

[31] In 1997, the PRI lost its absolute majority in the Chamber of Deputies for the first time in the party's history.

[32] In 1996, Eliseo Mendoza Berrueto (PRI), who had been a senator, governor, undersecretary, and Chamber majority leader in the 1980s, wrote that it

was a fact that the president was the chief of the party and that he had a decisive influence in the party's nomination of deputies, senators, and governors (see Eliseo Mendoza Berrueto, *El Presidencialismo mexicano: Génesis de un sistema imperfecto* [Mexico City: Fondo de Cultura Económica and Colegio de la Frontera Norte, 1996], p. 222).

[33] See Mayhew, *Congress: The Electoral Connection.*

[34] See Nacif-Hernández, "La No Reelección legislativa"; Alonso Lujambio "La Reelección de los legisladores: Las Ventajas y los dilemas," *Quórum*, January 1996; and Ugalde, "Consideraciones sobre la reelección en México."

[35] See Casar, "Las Relaciones entre el Poder Ejecutivo y el Legislativo"; and Nacif-Hernández, "La No Reelección legislativa."

[36] See North, *Institutions, Institutional Change, and Economic Performance*, chap. 1.

[37] For Centeno, "assuming that access to power is central to a politician's agenda, no-re-election deprived elite members of a means to power, independent of central control. If they could not be expected to be reelected, there was no incentive for them to cultivate a popular constituency. Why provide services to voters who could not return such favors with electoral support?" (see Centeno, *Democracy Within Reason*, p. 40).

[38] According to a poll conducted by *Fundación Arturo Rosenbluth*, 78 percent of Mexicans think that Congress has a key responsibility to oversee the honesty and efficiency of the government in collecting and spending public resources ($N = 1,500$).

[39] According to Casar, the factors that led deputies to act in the president's interest, and thus in their own, were the existence of a centralized party that controlled nominations from above, a unitary actor heading both the presidency and the party, the nonconsecutive reelection clause, and the existence of a spoils system in the hands of the chief executive. It is through this process that the president of Mexico was able to "penetrate" Congress and alter deputies' behavior and motivations, which eroded legislative authority and oversight capacity, on the one hand, and increased the controlling sphere of the presidency over the other branches of government, on the other hand. For Casar, the Constitution grants Congress sufficient authority to control the executive branch; in practice, the lack of control actually exerted could be explained by the president's "penetration" of Congress (see Casar, "Las Bases politico-institucionales," pp. 78–85).

[40] See Alicia Hernández Chavez, "La Parábola del presidencialismo mexicano," in *Presidencialismo y sistema político: México y los Estados Unidos*, ed. Alicia Hernández Chávez (Mexico City: Colegio de México and Fondo de Cultura Económica, 1994).

[41] See Luis F. Aguilar Villanueva, "El Presidencialismo y el sistema político Mexicano: Del Presidencialismo a la presidencia democrática," in Hernández Chávez, ed., ibid.

[42] See Orozco Henríquez, "El Sistema presidencial en el constituyente de Querétaro," p. 34.

[43] See Lujambio, "Adios a la excepcionalidad," p. 5. According to Osornio Corres, the strengthening of the presidential institution was part of a historical phase that built political institutions and ended the political unrest of the *caudillista* era. The author wrote that the president was far from being legally balanced by the other two branches of government, but that there had been some steps taken to strengthen the latter, including the enlargement of the Chamber of Deputies to 500 members, the double period of congressional sessions, the renewal of half of the Senate's members every three years, and the creation of the Court for Electoral Issues (see Francisco J. Osornio Corres, "Estructura funcional y orgánica del Ejecutivo Federal en México," in *El Sistema presidencial mexicano*, pp. 159–61).

[44] Mexico City is the most important state-level government in political and economic terms, and it has the budgetary resources and the size to reward loyal followers. The removal of Mexico City's mayor from the sphere of presidential appointees was sudden, because the first elected mayor happened to be a member of the PRD, an opposition party that was antagonistic to the PRI and to the chief executive. The mayor's inauguration brought to an end the vast array of resources available for presidential promotions.

[45] The governorship had been in the hands of a PAN member (Francisco Barrio), thus the result added visibility to the PRI democratic experiment.

CHAPTER SIX

STRENGTH OF THE OPPOSITION

WHEN THE INSTITUTIONAL REVOLUTIONARY PARTY LOST ITS absolute majority in the Chamber of Deputies in 1997 and President Zedillo had to face closer scrutiny and stronger opposition from Congress—after decades in which the PRI-controlled legislative branch had tacitly passed the president's bills without amendments—the logic and nature of relations between the executive and legislative branches of the Mexican government were altered forever, and the relationship between both branches became more balanced. In July 2000, the electorate decided to expand the experience of a divided government and even to reverse the players: this time voters elected a National Action Party candidate (Vicente Fox) to the presidency but did not vote in his party as a majority in Congress. With the PRI as the largest minority party in both houses and a PAN president, an even more balanced relationship between Congress and the presidency will be achieved. These developments support the hypothesis that the stronger the opposition in Congress, the more frequent legislative oversight will be.

Before 1997, the nonreelectability of deputies—combined with the partisan powers of the president—resulted in the alignment of PRI deputies' preferences with those of the executive branch, thereby limiting legislators' incentives to monitor the executive branch. When the PRI enjoyed comfortable majorities in the House, deputies' preferences easily became Chamber decisions. Conversely, when the PRI's strength in the Chamber began to decline, its ability to translate its preferences into legislative action (or lack thereof) also decreased.

For several decades, the PRI held not only an absolute majority in the Chamber of Deputies (above 50 percent) but also a "qualified" majority (above 66 percent). As political competitiveness grew and new electoral rules allowed votes to be fairly and proportionately translated into seats, the composition of the Chamber began to change dramatically.[1] Over the period of study, the PRI went from a position of hegemony in Congress in the early 1970s (more than 80 percent of Chamber seats) to one of dominance in the 1980s (about 65 percent of the seats). In the mid-1990s, the party's presence dropped to an absolute majority (just above 50 percent of the seats); and by 1997, the PRI had become the largest minority in the Chamber (47 percent of the seats). With the election in July 2000, the PRI lost its majority in the Senate but has remained as the largest minority in both houses.

CHAMBER AND COMMITTEE COMPOSITION, 1970–2000

From 1970 to 1988, the PRI held an average of 78 percent of the seats in the Chamber; in 1988, its share dropped to 52 percent; and from then on the party was never able to regain its qualified majority. In 1997, the PRI lost its absolute majority, as its share of seats dropped to a then historic low of 47 percent, making it the largest minority in the Chamber. With the congressional session beginning in fall 2000, the PRI's presence in the House decreased to 42 percent. Table 6.1 presents a detailed breakdown of the composition of the Chamber between 1970 and August 2003.

The share of party seats on congressional committees over that time period closely resembled that in the Chamber, although occasionally a gap could be observed. In general, the opposition's presence on committees was marginal in the early 1970s. Ten years later, the opposition managed to increase its membership by 25–35 percent per committee. With the upsurge in the opposition's numbers in the Chamber in 1997, the committees also came to be dominated by

Table 6.1
Party Composition of the Chamber of Deputies, 1970–2003
(in percent)

Legislature	PRI	PAN	PRD–Left[a]	Other[b]
1970–1973	83.5	9.3	7.0	0
1973–1976	81.8	10.8	7.3	0
1976–1979	81.7	8.5	9.7	0
1979–1982	74.5	10.7	12.2	2.5
1982–1985	74.7	12.6	9.5	3.0
1985–1988	72.0	10.2	14.7	3.0
1988–1991	52.2	20.2	27.6	0
1991–1994	65.4	17.6	7.2	0
1994–1997	60.2	23.6	14.0	0
1997–2000	47.6	24.2	26.6[c]	1.2[d]
2000–2003	42.2	41.2	10.0	6.6[e]
Average	**66.9**	**17.2**	**13.2**	**1.4**

[a] The PRD congressional group has existed as such since the 1991–94 Legislature. For previous legislatures, former leftist parties (which no longer exist) have been included (PPS, PCM, PMS, PRT, PMT, PSUM, PARM). These parties were, in some way or another, the forerunners to the PRD, which was formed in the early 1990s.
[b] Includes the Mexican Democracy Party and independents.
[c] Includes the Labor Party.
[d] Seats held by the Green Party.
[e] Includes the Green Party, Labor Party, Democratic Convergence Party, National Society Party, and Social Action Party
Source: Campos, "Un Congreso sin congresistas," p. 50.

opposition deputies, who then accounted for approximately 52 percent of most committee seats. However, the PRI managed to maintain a greater influence and share of committee leadership positions, as compared with the party's strength in the House. It was only in the early 1990s that the opposition was able to gain a presence in these leadership positions.

The PRI's presence on the Budget Committee was reduced from complete dominance in the 1970s to the largest minority in 1997. At the leadership level (chair, or *presidencia,* and the second-ranking position, *secretaría),* the PRI was able to maintain its overrepresentation. Indeed, until 1991, the Budget Committee had always been led by *priístas*, with no opposition member occupying either leadership position. From 1991 to 1997, the leadership was enlarged with the addition of more *secretaríos*, but the chair remained filled by PRI members. However, in 1997, as part of the negotiations to install the new legislature in which—for the first time—the PRI did not hold an absolute majority, the opposition demanded and got the position of chair of the Budget Committee.[2] Table 6.2 provides a detailed breakdown of the composition of the Budget Committee between 1970 and 2000.

The composition of the Supervisory Committee generally followed the pattern found in the Chamber, and its leadership was traditionally dominated by the PRI. The leadership had always been *priísta* before 1991, the year in which opposition deputies were included as *secretaríos*, but the chair remained occupied by PRI members. A historic change occurred in 1994: Juan Antonio García Villa, a member of the PAN, was chosen to chair the committee as part of negotiations to install the new legislature prior to the inauguration of President Zedillo's administration. The chair remained in the opposition's control for the next legislature (1997–2000), this time as part of the negotiations to install a new legislature in which the PRI was a minority for the first time.[3] (See table 6.3 for a detailed breakdown of the composition of the Supervisory Committee between 1997 and 2000.)

The leadership of the Supervisory Committee by a PAN member since 1994 has had a tremendous impact on the frequency of legislative oversight. This may constitute the most important single event to have directed attention to the importance of both this committee and the Treasury Accounting Office. Before 1994, the Supervisory Committee had been considered an ineffective vehicle for building political capital and gaining visibility within the Chamber. As a result of PAN leadership, however, it has now become one of the most visible and most attractive committees in the Chamber. According to 41 percent of the deputies interviewed, the change in the committee's leadership from a PRI member to an opposition member helped to improve oversight; 37 percent believed that the change

Table 6.2
Strength of the Opposition Within the Budget Committee, 1970–2000

Category	Legislature									
	70–73	73–76	76–79	79–82	82–85	85–88	88–91	91–94	94–97	97–00
Size	25	15	28	21	34	43	58	70	30	30
Party affiliation (in percent)										
PRI	88	100	92.9	76.2	76.5	65.1	63.8	77.1	60.0	46.6
Opposition	12	0	7.1	23.8	23.5	34.9	36.2	22.9	40.0	53.4
Leadership[a]										
PRI	2	2	2	2	2	2	3	3	3	1
Opposition	0	0	0	0	0	0	0	2	3	5[b]

[a] Leadership includes the committee chair (called *presidencia*) and the second-ranking positions (called *secretarios*).
[b] Includes the committee chair, which in 1997 was occupied for the first time in history by a non-PRI member (García Sainz from the PRD).

Sources: Diccionario biográfico del gobierno mexicano, various years; *Diary of Debates*, various years; Congressional Records, various years. For 1997–2000, see the Web site of the Chamber of Deputies: <http://www.cddhcu.gob.mx>.

Table 6.3
Strength of the Opposition Within the Supervisory Committee, 1970–2000

| Category | \\ Legislature | | | | | | | | | |
	70–73	73–76	76–79	79–82	82–85	85–88	88–91	91–94	94–97	97–00
Size	7	11	4	14	14	32	17	43	28	29
Party affiliation (in percent)										
PRI	100	100	100	64.3	64.3	59.4	64.7	76.7	60.7	48.2
Opposition	0	0	0	35.7	35.7	40.6	35.3	23.3	39.3	51.8
Leadership[a]										
PRI	2	2	2	2	2	2	2	2	2	1
Opposition	0	0	0	0	0	0	0	2	3[b]	3[b]

[a] Leadership includes the committee chair (called *presidencia*) and the second-ranking positions (called *secretarios*).

[b] Includes the committee chair, which in 1997 was occupied for the first time in history by a non-PRI member (García Sainz from the PRD).

Sources: Diccionario biográfico del gobierno mexicano, various years; *Diary of Debates,* various years; Congressional Records, various years. For 1997–2000, see the Web site of the Chamber of Deputies: <http://www.cddhcu.gob.mx>.

Table 6.4
PAN Chairmanship's Impact on the Supervisory Committee's Oversight Efforts, 1994–97
(opinions by party group)[a]
(in percent)
($N = 49$)

Position	Opinion by Party			Total
	PRI	PAN	PRD	
Oversight has improved	22.2	76.9	44.4	40.8
No impact at all	55.5	7.6	22.2	36.7
Oversight has worsened	11.1	0	0	4.0
No answer	14.8	15.3	33.3	18.3

[a] Question asked of deputies: In the 56th Legislature (1994–97), an opposition deputy chaired the Supervisory Committee for the first time in history (J. A. Garcia Villa). Has that fact had any impact on the oversight of the executive branch by the Chamber and the Treasury Accounting Office?
Source: Personal interviews.

had no impact at all; and only 4 percent thought that it made legislative oversight worse. The results of the interviews, shown in table 6.4, demonstrate the partisanship of the responses.

MOTIVATIONS OF OPPOSITION DEPUTIES

Until recently, political rationale in terms of career advancement was different for deputies from the opposition and those from the PRI. Because the political futures of opposition members were not linked to the president's will but to their party's support for nomination to elected office or appointment to a position within the party structure, opposition deputies carved their paths to higher office by overseeing and criticizing the chief executive's performance. How different were the motivations of PRI and opposition deputies? Did they differ enough to postulate two sets of motives within the Chamber—one for PRI deputies and one for non-*priístas*? The following pages will present data to help answer these questions.

Table 6.5
Likely Motivations of PAN Deputies, 1994–97
(opinions by party group)[a]
(1 = least important, 5 = most important)
($N = 49$)

Motivation	Opinion by Party			Weighted Average
	PRI	PAN	PRD	
To oversee and control the executive branch	4.2	4.5	4.0	4.2
To follow the party's mandate and program	4.5	4.0	3.8	4.1
To follow the Speaker's mandate and goals	4.5	3.5	3.9	4.1
To advance one's own political career	4.3	3.2	4.0	3.9
To carry out personal ideals and commitments	3.9	3.7	3.0	3.6
To discredit the actions of the administration	4.3	2.1	3.0	3.5
To fulfill voters' demands	1.9	3.6	2.5	2.4

Note: Shading indicates highest grades by party.
[a] Question asked of deputies: In your opinion, how important is each of the following motives in explaining the behavior of PAN deputies, on a scale 1–5, where 1 means that the motive is not important, and 5 means that the motive is very important.
Source: Personal interviews.

National Action Party Members' Motivations

To examine PAN deputies' motivations, interviews were conducted in which members of the three major parties were asked to provide their opinions about the likely motivations of PAN members (*panistas*), who were members of the opposition at the time. The main conclusions—as shown in table 6.5—are the following:

1. Deputies considered PAN members' primary motivation in the House to be oversight and control of the executive branch. For PRI deputies, however, this motivation ranked as the *least* important (as was shown in table 5.2 on page 132).

2. According to deputies, the next motivation for PAN members' actions—in order of reported importance—was to follow their party's mandate and program.

3. The next two motivations attributed to PAN members—to follow the Speaker's mandate and goals and to advance their political careers—received similar attention by *priístas* (as shown in table 5.2 on page 132).

4. A troubling similarity between PRI and PAN members was the low priority both parties attached to fulfilling voters' demands: in the case of PAN members, it ranked as the least important motivation.

Democratic Revolutionary Party Members' Motivations

The same process was followed in an effort to understand likely motivations of lawmakers from the Democratic Revolutionary Party. The main conclusions that can be drawn from the data shown in table 6.6 are the following:

1. Deputies considered that the PRD's most important motivation was to discredit the actions of the administration. The PRD differed drastically not only from the PRI on this point (not surprisingly) but also from the PAN (this motivation was seen as the second *least* important for *panistas*).

2. Advancing one's political career appeared as the second most important goal for PRD members, according to deputies' responses. This goal was shared to a similar degree by all deputies, regardless of party affiliation, a finding that reinforces the assumption made in chapter 4 of this book.

3. Oversight and control of the executive branch appeared as the next most sought-after goal attributed to the PRD, a goal the party shared with the PAN.

4. Deputies judged that the PRD was less motivated to follow the party's mandate and program as well as the Speaker's mandate and goals. Here the PRD differed from both the PRI and the PAN, for whom both goals were more relevant.

Table 6.6
Likely Motivations of PRD Deputies, 1994–97
(opinions by party group)[a]
(1 = least important, 5 = most important)
(N = 49)

Motivation	Opinion by Party			Weighted Average
	PRI	PAN	PRD	
To discredit the actions of the administration	4.9	4.8	4.1	**4.7**
To advance one's own political career	4.8	4.3	4.1	**4.5**
To oversee and control the executive branch	4.7	4.4	4.2	**4.5**
To carry out personal ideals and commitments	4.1	3.9	3.2	**3.8**
To follow the party's mandate and program	3.1	3.1	2.9	**3.0**
To follow the Speaker's mandate and goals	3.2	2.6	2.6	**2.9**
To fulfill voters' demands	2.4	3.2	2.5	**2.6**

Note: Shading indicates highest grades by party.

[a]Question asked of deputies: In your opinion, how important is each of the following motives in explaining the behavior of PRD deputies, on a scale 1–5, where 1 means not important, and 5 means very important?

Source: Personal interviews.

5. Another troubling similarity is evident: for the PRD, the fulfillment of voters' demands was also seen to be the least important
motivation behind its deputies' actions, even according to PRD
deputies themselves.

Comparison of All Deputies' Motivations

In order to compare the motivations of members of all three parties,
the deputies' responses to questions on this issue were ranked and aggregated, as shown in table 6.7. According to the responses to the
questions that were posed, oversight and control of the executive
branch was the highest priority of PAN and PRD deputies (an average

Table 6.7
Likely Motivations of All Deputies, 1994–97
(opinions by all party groups aggregated)[a]
(1 = least important, 5 = most important)
(N = 49)

Motivation	Opinion by Party			Weighted Average[b]
	PRI	PAN	PRD	
To advance one's own political career	4.2	2.4	4.5	4.2
To follow the Speaker's mandate and goals	4.4	4.1	2.9	4.0
To follow the party's mandate and program	4.0	4.1	3.0	3.8
To carry out personal ideals and commitments	3.3	3.6	3.8	3.5
To oversee and control the executive branch	1.8	4.2	4.5	2.9
To fulfill voters' demands	2.1	2.4	2.6	2.3

Note: Shading indicates highest grades by party.
[a] Question asked of deputies: How important is each of the following motives in explaining the behavior of PRI, PAN, and PRD deputies, on a scale 1–5, where 1 means not important, and 5 means very important.
[b] Weighted according to share of interviewees' party.
Source: See tables 5.2, 6.5, and 6.6.

of 4.2 and 4.5, respectively). But because *priístas* averaged a score of only 1.8 on that goal, its overall importance to all deputies decreased accordingly—to a weighted average of only 2.9. If the opposition had had a larger share of seats, their greater desire for oversight would certainly have been reflected in more legislative action on this issue.

To assess how the motivations of each party's members might translate into an aggregated preference of all Chamber members (if that sort of thing existed), each motivation shown in table 6.7 was weighted according to the relative share of Chamber seats held by each party between 1970 and 2000. For that purpose, three periods were established:

1. The *inconsequential* period, 1970–88, in which all opposition parties combined held an average of 22 percent of the seats in the Chamber;

2. The *minority* period, 1988–97, in which the opposition held an average of 41 percent of Chamber seats; and

3. The *majority* period, 1997–2000, in which the opposition en bloc had an absolute majority of 52 percent.

Aggregating the scores and weighting them by party share of Chamber seats demonstrates how the relative importance of each motivation could have evolved over time as a result of the changes in the Chamber's composition. In other words, as the opposition gained seats, it also increased its ability to turn preferences into legislative action. Even though this example is speculative and has no statistical significance, it does suggest the relative weight partisanship can have in legislative decisionmaking.

In analyzing the scores, it is obvious that, in general, the values of each motivation did not change sharply as the opposition got stronger, except in one case. Oversight and control of the executive branch increased its value by almost 35 percent between 1970 and 1997. The remaining values varied within a range of 10 points. The results presented in table 6.8 indicate that legislative oversight was positively correlated with the strength of the opposition, as suggested by the hypothesis of this study.

STRENGTH OF THE OPPOSITION AND ITS EFFECT ON LEGISLATIVE OVERSIGHT

Chapters 2 and 3 of this book provided ample descriptions of the way legislative oversight was conducted between 1970 and 1999. The examples given described the approval of the budget bill, the review and revision of the Public Account, the auditing process of the Treasury Accounting Office, and the creation of investigative committees. In order to probe the possible correlation between the strength of the opposition and the frequency of oversight activities, the information discussed in earlier chapters has been condensed and is presented in table 6.9, which offers a comprehensive view of how party

Table 6.8
Evolution of Deputies' Motivations, 1970–2000
(by periods, according to strength of the opposition)
(1 = least important, 5 = most important)

| Motivation | Period | | | Percentage Change, 1970–2000 |
	1970–88 Inconsequential (Opposition About 22%)	1988–97 Minority (Opposition About 40%)	1997–2000 Majority (Opposition en Bloc Above 50%)	
To advance one's own political career	4.0	3.7	3.8	-5.0
To follow the Speaker's mandate and goals	4.1	3.9	3.9	-4.8
To follow the party's mandate and program	3.8	3.7	3.7	-2.6
To carry out personal ideals and commitments	3.3	3.3	3.5	6.0
To oversee and control the executive branch	2.3	2.7	3.1	34.7
To fulfill voters' demands	2.1	2.2	2.3	9.5

Source: See tables 6.1 and 6.7.

composition of the Chamber may have affected the amount of oversight conducted. In general, the frequency and visibility of legislative oversight increased along with the growth in the opposition's share of House seats. The conclusions that are the most relevant to the topic of this study are discussed in the sections that follow.

Budget Bills

Between 1970 and 1987, the budget bills submitted by the executive branch were not changed, except on two occasions, and even those changes were not substantial. During the period 1988–96, the Chamber began to introduce changes of minor importance but did not modify the substance and guidelines of the budget (as detailed in table 2.1 on pages 27–28). However, over the last three years—the period when the opposition held a majority in the House—major and previously unthinkable modifications were made. As an example, the 1999 budget bill, submitted in November 1998, was completely modified by the Chamber; so many changes were made that the administration's initial reaction was to reject the proposals. However, the strength of the opposition and the possibility that the budget bill would not be approved by the deadline mandated for approval exerted such pressure that the government conceded at the last minute and the bill was passed just hours before the beginning of the fiscal year. The approval of the 1999 budget constitutes the first example of how the Chamber can exert the "power of the purse."[4] The 2000 budget bill faced a similar situation (as described in detail in chapter 2 of this book).

Public Attention to Legislative Oversight

Legislative oversight has only recently begun to receive public attention. In the early 1990s, little attention was paid to the work of the Supervisory Committee and the Treasury Accounting Office. Membership on the committee was small, and its chairs were usually held by relatively insignificant deputies. Things began to change in 1994, when a PAN member was chosen to chair the committee. The committee began to hold more meetings, started to publish the results of audits conducted by the Treasury Accounting Office, requested cooperation from government agencies in matters related to oversight, and denounced agencies that obstructed legislative oversight. Over the 1970–87 period, the Supervisory Committee was referred to an average of 142 times a year during floor debates; for the 1988–96 period, the figure jumped to 420 annual references, indicating a significant increase in its activities and the attention its work received. The same pattern can be observed in press coverage of the committee's work (see table 2.8 on page 53 and table 6.9).

Investigative Committees

Finally, a similar pattern is evident in the case of investigative committees. Between 1978 and 1987, only one committee was requested

Table 6.9
Frequency of Legislative Oversight and Major Oversight Activities, 1970–99 (selected years)

Period	Budget		Public Account	CMH Audits per Year[c]	Public Attention to Legislative Oversight		Investigative Committees	
	Changes to Original Bill	Votes Against[a]	Votes Against[b]		References in Diary of Debates[d]	References in Press[e]	Requested but not Created	Requested and Created
1970–87								
1970	No	0	10	—	32	41	f	f
1972	No	10	8	—	32	—	f	f
1976	No	0	9	—	40	—	f	f
1978	No	0	9	47	158	37	0	0
1979	No	19	—	67	158	—	0	1
1980	No	21	16	23	158	—	0	0
1982	No	23	20	185	230	—	0	0
1984	No	3	—	390	280	—	0	0
1986	Minor[g]	25	20	390	280	45	0	0
1987	No	17	17	391	266	—	0	0
Average	NO	10.3	14.1	159	142	41	Total 0	1
1988–96								
1988	Minor[g]	40	—	342	266	—	2	0
1989	No	16	35	—	266	—	0	1
1990	Minor[g]	35	23	393	409	53	1	0
1992	Minor[g]	20	26	500	529	—	1	0
1995	Minor[g]	—	35	—	—	49	0	1
1996	No	—	35	—	—	—	1	0
Average	MINOR[g]	24.3	29.8	463	420	51	Total 5	Total 2

Table 6.9
Continued

Period	Budget		Public Account	CMH Audits per Year[c]	Public Attention to Legislative Oversight		Investigative Committees	
	Changes to Original Bill	Votes Against[a]	Votes Against[b]		References in Diary of Debates[d]	References in Press[e]	Requested but not Created	Requested and Created
1997–99								
1997	Major[g]	26	—	726	—	—	0	1
1998	Major[g]	28	2	—	—	83	0	1
1999	Major[g]	2	—	—	—	—	0	2
Average	MAJOR	18.6	2	726	—	83 Total	0 Total	4

[a] Votes against budget bills as an indicator of the level of attention given to ex-ante oversight.

[b] Votes against the Public Account as an indicator of dissatisfaction with the way legislative oversight used to be conducted.

[c] Annual audits conducted by the Treasury Accounting Office as an indicator of the frequency of oversight activities.

[d] The *Diary of Debates* is an internal House record and reflects the attention received within the House.

[e] *El Universal,* September–December of the years indicated.

[f] Constitutional Article 93, Paragraph 3, which is the legal foundation for these committees, was promulgated in 1977; therefore, 1978 is the first year in which such committees could have been requested and formed.

[g] Minor changes mean small modifications to secondary items that are not significant in the overall budget. Major changes mean extensive modifications to significant items in the budget (see table 2.1).

Sources: For Budget columns, see tables 2.1 and 2.2; for Public Account votes, see table 2.5; for CMH audits, see table 2.7; for references in *Diary of Debates,* relevant years; and for references in the press, see *El Universal,* September–December of the relevant years.

and created, despite the fact that minority parties had a constitutional right to do so (as discussed in chapter 3). During the subsequent period, 1988–96, seven committees were requested, but only two were actually created. Finally, in the course of the last three years, four committees were requested and created: (1) the second CONASUPO Committee, a committee that had been created in 1995, shut down by the PRI group in 1996, and reopened in 1997; (2) the Mexican Institute for Social Security Committee, created in 1998 to investigate the operation and reform program of the Social Security Institute; (3) the CFE and LFC Committee, which was created in April 1999 to investigate the functioning of state-owned power plants; and (4) the *Nacional Financiera* Committee, created at the end of 1999 to investigate the retirement and pension program provided to high-level officials within the state-owned development bank.

The breakdown of legislative oversight activities outlined in table 6.9 supports the hypothesis that the greater the strength of the opposition in the Chamber, the more frequent the oversight activities carried out by the legislature. Each of the numbers in the table reflects the tendency for oversight to increase as the opposition's presence in the Chamber grows stronger. With the larger presence of the opposition in the new Congress, which took office in September 2000—this time with the PRI as an opposition party—it is likely that congressional oversight will expand. However, the outcome will partly depend on the behavior of the PAN congressional delegation in its dealings with the newly elected president, himself a member of the same party.

As stated in this book's introductory chapter, legislative oversight in Mexico is beginning to undergo major changes. The long period during which Congress neither mattered nor paid attention to government actions has come to an end. Today, the Chamber of Deputies is monitoring every step the administration takes, unfortunately not always with the qualified human capital and resources that these activities require. Nevertheless, at least the Mexican Congress has begun to assert its determination to oversee the government of the republic.

Notes

[1] For a historical review of electoral systems in Mexico and its reforms, see Juan Molinar Horcasitas, *El Tiempo de la legitimidad: Elecciones, autoritarismo y democracia en México* (Mexico City: Cal y Arena, 1991). Recent reforms can be viewed on the Federal Electoral Institute's Web site at <www.ife.gob.mx>.

[2] The internal rules guiding the formation of committees are quite ambiguous. Indeed, only recently was the size of the committees regulated for the first time. Before that, discretion and ad hoc solutions tended to prevail when committees were being formed. Table 6.2 shows how both the size of the Budget Committee and its leadership have varied over time. Most of these variations were responses to the political necessity of allocating leadership and membership positions among as many deputies as possible, even if they did not represent any real influence in decisionmaking. For a discussion of the impact of the internal rules of the Chamber on the functioning of committees, see Nacif-Hernández, "The Mexican Chamber of Deputies," chaps. 4 and 5.

[3] Part of the explanation for the absence of opposition deputies on the Supervisory Committee before 1991 lies in the fact that the committee lacked visibility among incoming deputies. Because legislative oversight had been dismissed as unimportant, membership was not considered politically attractive. This also explains the low membership on the Supervisory Committee compared with other committees (such as the Budget Committee). In 1976–79, for example, the Supervisory Committee had only 4 members while the Budget Committee had 28; in 1988–91 it had only 17 members while Budget had 58 (see tables 6.2 and 6.3).

[4] Among other changes, the administration's expenditures were reduced by 20 percent; fiscal transfers to state and municipal governments were increased by 10 percent; and funding for the legislative and judicial branches was cut by 4 percent.

CHAPTER SEVEN

CONCLUSION

PAST PROBLEMS AND FUTURE CHALLENGES

THE SITUATION TODAY

Mexico's political landscape has changed dramatically over the past several years. Even though democracy was not born in July 2000—when an opposition candidate won the presidency for the first time in Mexico's modern history—that event has shown that Mexico's electoral democracy is a reality, albeit with some weaknesses and imperfections. For most of the period during which the Institutional Revolutionary Party controlled the presidency, a recurrent concern was the concentration of power in the executive branch and the submissive role played by Congress, both of which impeded the emergence of a true system of checks and balances.

For most of the years between 1970 and 2000, the Mexican Chamber of Deputies did not take full advantage of its constitutional authority to oversee and control the government's executive branch. Although the Constitution and other laws grant the Chamber sufficient powers to monitor the activities of the government, in practice there has been a gap between what the written norm establishes and the amount and type of legislative oversight that have actually been conducted. (As table 7.1 shows, deputies themselves ranked the efficacy of their oversight as either "average" or "poor.") With the shift in political power resulting from the July 2000 election, a pertinent concern is the role the new Congress will play in overseeing and controlling the executive branch.

Table 7.1
Efficacy of Legislative Oversight, 1994–97
(as perceived by deputies)[a]
($N = 49$)

Degree of Efficacy	Opinion by Party			Weighted Average
	PRI	PAN	PRD	
Very Good	0	0	0	0
Good	11.1	15.3	0	10.2
Average	44.4	38.4	22.2	38.7
Poor	33.3	38.4	77.7	42.8
Very Poor	11.1	7.6	0	8.1
Weighted Grade[b]	5.1	5.2	4.4	5.2

[a] Question asked of deputies: Today, how do you evaluate the efficacy of the oversight and control of the executive branch performed by the Chamber of Deputies?
[b] Very good = 10; good = 8; average = 6; poor = 4; very poor = 2.
Source: Personal interviews.

Monitoring government expenditures is one of the principal areas defining the relationship between the executive and legislative branches of government in Mexico, as it is in most countries of the world. The data and opinions of current and former deputies that were collected and analyzed for this study indicate that the Chamber of Deputies' supervision of public spending over most of the 1970–2000 period was both insufficient and ineffective. In addition, data collected from the archives of the Treasury Accounting Office and the Chamber's Supervisory Committee reflect deputies' lack of competence in overseeing government expenditures. Legislative oversight frequently lacked standard operating procedures, government agencies often failed to comply with the Chamber's requests for information, and deputies did not even monitor the prosecution of cases or the enforcement of rules governing oversight.

It would be incorrect to argue that insufficient and weak legislative oversight was the cause of government corruption. It is reasonable to suggest, however, that lack of adequate and prompt supervision did, by omission, contribute to the "impunity" and lack of account-ability that characterized the functioning of the executive branch over the period of study. In turn, lack of accountability on the part of the executive branch facilitated its misconduct and corruption.

Over the last several years, especially since 1997, the frequency of legislative oversight has increased, as has the Chamber's criticism of cases of government mismanagement and corruption. Although the effectiveness of the Chamber's oversight efforts is still very limited, the fact that the Chamber has begun to exercise its legal authority to control the administration and review its financial operations has contributed to the increase in the government's accountability to the Mexican people. In turn, this has contributed to the creation of proactive controls that eventually will manage to prevent or at least minimize the government's misconduct.

LIKELY CAUSES

Many factors can explain the infrequency and ineffectiveness of legis-lative oversight in Mexico. According to deputies' opinions, as indi-cated in table 5.3 on page 134, the most relevant variables fall within the category of motivational factors, followed in importance by ca-pability factors. Although staff support and legal institutions (that is, structural factors) play a role in explaining the weakness of legis-lative supervision, their weight is relatively unimportant in com-parison to the first two types.

Motivational factors seem to be the leading cause behind the weak legislative oversight that was observed. In particular, PRI deputies showed a pattern of behavior that was designed to protect the presi-dent from criticism by the opposition and to avoid any action that could have interfered with the government's functioning or been per-ceived as a threat to the administration. This behavior was especially acute before 1997, when the PRI always held majorities in both houses of Congress and the president's partisan powers were stronger.

The reversed-accountability hypothesis explains PRI deputies' unwillingness to hold the executive branch accountable for its ac-tions: doing so would have impeded the advancement of their politi-cal careers, which was one of their incentives. On the one hand, the "electoral" connection between legislators and their constituents was—and still is—weak as a result of the Constitution's nonconsecutive reelection clause. The inability to reward good performance with reelection renders voters irrelevant in terms of the career development of their representatives. On the other hand, during the period of this study, the president's partisan powers enabled him to promote the careers of outgoing PRI deputies. Consequently, legislators' political responsibility was inverted from their constituents to the chief executive.

Because the PRI held a majority of seats in the Chamber until 1997, PRI deputies' preferences and motivations prevailed over the goals of other groups in the Chamber. The result was a weak and ineffective pattern of legislative oversight of public expenditures and executive actions. This lack of *will* to oversee the administration was compounded by the absence of a cadre of experienced and competent deputies (labeled as a capability factor). As table 4.5 on page 106 shows, deputies themselves indicated that they evaluated the overall professional quality of lawmakers as being average to low, with a weighted grade of 5.6 on a 10-point scale, with 10 indicating "very high." Nonreelectability of members of Congress limited their experience within the Chamber, reduced the stimulus for lawmakers to specialize in committee work, and kept competent politicians out of the Chamber. Insufficient experience of deputies was almost built into the system, because they were unable to build careers out of their Chamber seats (most incoming deputies in each legislature had never held a seat before). Lack of specialization was assured because of the absence of incentives to devote the resources needed to acquire the expertise afforded by serving on oversight committees: neither oversight nor specialization was considered to be politically rewarding. The limited professionalism of deputies resulted partly from the need to recruit less-qualified deputies because of the relative unattractiveness and low prestige of the Chamber, which was perceived as only a temporary step in political advancement, not a long-term goal in itself.

Lack of incentives to oversee the administration (a motivational cause) plus a low level of professional quality and experience on the part of those responsible for oversight (a capability cause), combined to enfeeble deputies' willingness and their capacity to monitor government activities over most of the period under study. The situation has changed in recent years, however. Legislators have become increasingly more motivated to oversee the administration, mainly as a result of the experience of a divided government that began in 1997. As the opposition has increased its share of Chamber seats, its influence in monitoring government activities has expanded accordingly. In 1997, the opposition—en bloc—became a majority in the Chamber for the first time in Mexican history. This shift led to unprecedented controls: the last two budget bills, for example, have undergone major changes, and the Chamber has begun to play a role in making corruption more visible, even to the point of contributing to the prosecution of government officials.

As a newly elected government takes office in December 2000, the experience of divided government will expand, because the share of opposition seats in Congress will be larger than ever before. This time, however, the PRI will form part of the opposition, while a National Action Party president will lead the executive branch. Therefore, instances of legislative oversight will likely increase as a result of the opposition's strength in Congress. But the impact of the reversal of actors in charge of both the presidency and the Congress remains open to conjecture.

Unfortunately, increased incentives for legislative oversight have not been accompanied by an equal increase in the capability and resources to perform the required tasks effectively. As the Mexican experience has shown, greater determination to supervise is not automatically translated into an effective mechanism for controlling the executive branch. The gap between motivations and capabilities must be closed, or the Mexican Congress will have a strong voice but not enough power and expertise to influence public policy and to control the actions of government effectively. If Congress does not enact further reforms, the shift in power may turn out to be disappointing in terms of creating a true system of checks and balances.

The gradual curtailment of the president's power to promote the careers of loyal supporters also contributed to increased legislative supervision, albeit to a lesser extent. On the one hand, President Zedillo partially relinquished his partisan powers, especially those that allowed him to select candidates for governorships and, to a lesser extent, candidates for the presidency. In doing so, he rendered the presidency less attractive as a focal point for promoting the careers of Mexican politicians. And with PRI candidate Francisco Labastida's loss in his bid for the presidency, the president's partisan powers have ceased to exist. On the other hand, President Zedillo had fewer resources at his disposal to implement his promotion powers: the number of elected offices controlled by the PRI and the streamlining of the public sector afforded fewer bureaucratic opportunities to attract and reward supporters and to exercise political patronage.

THE ROLE OF CONGRESS IN THE POLITICAL MODERNIZATION OF MEXICO

The consolidation of Mexican democracy passes through two rounds of political reforms. The first, already completed, refers to electoral reforms that allow citizens' preferences to be translated into votes and elected representatives. This is the input side of democracy. Once elected, politicians are constantly faced with the temptation to disregard their mandate and govern in their own interests, or on behalf of interest groups with whom they are allied. Therefore, it is imperative to establish additional control mechanisms to ensure that elected officials, especially those in the executive branch, will perform their duties honestly and efficiently while simultaneously pursuing policies aimed at the public good. This is the output side of democracy. Regular elections can induce some sort of accountability, but the main vehicle for guaranteeing political responsibility, efficiency, and honesty on the part of elected public officials remains in the hands of Congress.

With the increase in the political strength of opposition parties under PRI presidents, especially between 1997 and 2000, Congress gained a stronger voice, but it lacked an adequate institutional framework to translate this impetus into actual and effective legislative oversight. As pluralism becomes the rule rather than the exception, a new set of standards needs to be designed that will enable Congress to be a professional and effective participant in national politics. In the realm of formal institutions, the following steps need to be taken:

1. Article 59 of the Constitution must be reformed to provide for consecutive reelection of deputies and senators, but with established term limits.

2. The exclusive and concurrent powers of both chambers must be revised, especially in matters related to the approval of the federal budget.

3. Budgetary legislation must be revised in a way that will clarify the legal controversies that have plagued the formation of investigative committees.

4. The functioning of investigative committees must be regulated.

5. Deputies must be allocated additional financial resources and staff; the Chamber at large requires better access to information and technological resources, and the new *Auditoría Superior de la Federación* will also need more human resources as well as technological ones.

It is important to note that politicians are rational individuals, not moral agents. Criticizing the passivity of the Mexican Congress during recent decades from the standpoint of morality is irrelevant. What matters is not the political beliefs of members of Congress, but the institutions—both formal and informal—that regulate and motivate their behavior. The institutional framework regulating relations between the executive and legislative branches of the Mexican government during the twentieth century hindered timely and effective congressional oversight, which could have counterbalanced the executive branch. Therefore, changing this set of rules can alter the behavior and characteristics of deputies recruited into the Chamber. Informal institutions have already changed, because the PRI will no longer exert the unified control of the executive and legislative branches as it once did. It is the formal institutions that now remain in need of change (along the lines recommended above).

The PRI has often been accused of having distorted congressional oversight efforts. This criticism would have probably been raised against any party that had maintained unified control of the presidency and Congress for such an extended period. Therefore, future political reforms in Mexico should be passed along nonpartisan lines, accompanied by a long-term perspective, so that a system of checks and balances can be developed and institutionalized, regardless of which party controls the presidency or Congress, or both. As soon as electoral reforms have had an impact on the democratization of Mexico, it will be up to the Mexican Congress to exercise its role in consolidating the country's democracy.

BIBLIOGRAPHY

BOOKS AND ARTICLES

Aberbach, Joel D. *Keeping a Watchful Eye: The Politics of Congressional Oversight.* Washington, D.C.: The Brookings Institution, 1990.

Adam, Alfredo, and Guillermo Becerril. *La Fiscalización en México.* First reprint. Mexico City: Universidad Nacional Autónoma de México, 1996.

Aguilar Camín, Héctor. *Después del milagro.* Mexico: Cal y Arena, 1991.

Aguilar Camín, Héctor, and Lorenzo Meyer. *A la Sombra de la Revolución Mexicana.* Mexico City: Cal y Arena, 1989.

Aguilar Villanueva, Luis F. "El Presidencialismo y el sistema político mexicano: Del Presidencialismo a la presidencia democrática." In *Presidencialismo y sistema político: México y los Estados Unidos,* edited by Alicia Hernández Chávez. Mexico City: Colegio de México and Fondo de Cultura Económica, 1994.

Alchian, Armen, and Harold Demsetz. "Production, Information Costs, and Economic Organization." *American Economic Review* 62 (1972): 777–95.

Arnaut, Alberto. "El Partido Nacional Revolucionario y la no-reelección consecutiva de legisladores." Paper presented at a meeting entitled La No-Reelección Consecutiva de los Legisladores y el Sistema Político Mexicano, Centro de Investigación y Docencia Económicas, Mexico City, March 11, 1996.

Arnold, R. Douglas. "Political Control of Administrative Officials." *Journal of Law, Economics, and Organizations* 3 (1987): 279–86.

Banks, Jeffrey S. "Agency Budgets, Cost Information, and Auditing." *American Journal of Political Science* 33 (1989): 670–99.

Banks, Jeffrey S, and Barry R. Weingast. "The Political Control of Bureaucracies under Asymmetric Information." *American Journal of Political Science* 36 (1992): 507–24.

Barquín Alvarez, Manuel. "Comentario al Artículo 59." In Cámara de Diputados, 55 Legislatura, *Derechos del pueblo mexicano: México a través de sus Constituciones*, Vol. 9. Mexico City: Cámara de Diputados, 1994.

———. "El Control del Senado sobre el Ejecutivo: Un Equilibrio oscilante de poderes." In *Estudios jurídicos en torno a la Constitución Mexicana de 1917, en su Septuagésimo Quinto Aniversario*. Mexico City: Instituto de Investigaciones Jurídicas, Universidad Nacional Autónoma de México, 1992.

———. "El Control parlamentario sobre el Ejecutivo desde una perspectiva comparativa." *Revista Mexicana de Estudios Parlamentarios*, January–April 1991.

Bawn, Kathleen. "Institutional Arrangements and Legislative Behavior: The Politics of Institutional Choice." Ph.D. diss., Stanford University, 1992.

———. "Political Control versus Expertise: Congressional Choice about Administrative Procedures." *American Political Science Review* 89 (1995).

Bazdrech, Carlos, et al., eds. *Lecturas 73 del trimestre económico— México: Auge, crisis y ajuste I*. Mexico City: Fondo de Cultura Económica, 1992.

Béjar, Luisa A. "El Control de la Asamblea de Representantes sobre el gobierno del Distrito Federal." *Asamblea* 4, no.7 (August 1995).

———. "El Legislativo en el sistema político mexicano." *Crónica Legislativa*, n.s., 3, no. 14 (1994): 43–45.

———. "La Reelección parlamentaria en México." *Asamblea* 4, no. 4 (May 1995).

Blum Valenzuela, Roberto. *De la Política mexicana y sus medios: Deterioro institucional o nuevo pacto político?* Mexico City:

Centro de Investigación para el Desarrollo, A.C., and Editorial Miguel Angel Porrúa, 1996.

Brandenburg, Frank Ralph. *The Making of Modern Mexico.* Englewood Cliffs, N.J.: Prentice-Hall, 1964.

Burgoa, Ignacio. *Breve Estudio sobre el Poder Legislativo.* Mexico City, 1966.

Calvert, Randall L., Mathew D. McCubbins, and Barry R. Weingast. "A Theory of Political Control and Bureaucratic Discretion." *American Journal of Political Science*, 33 (August 1989): 588–611.

Camacho Solís, Manuel. "Los Nudos históricos del sistema político mexicano." In *Las Crisis en el sistema político mexicano, 1928–1977.* Mexico City: Colegio de México, 1977.

Camp, Roderic A. "Mexico's Legislature: Missing the Democratic Lockstep?" In *Legislatures and the New Democracies in Latin America*, edited by David Close. Boulder, Colo.: Lynne Reinner Publishers, 1995.

Campos, Emma. "Un Congreso sin congresistas: La No-Reelección consecutiva en el Poder Legislativo mexicano, 1934–1997." B.A. thesis, Instituto Tecnológico Autónomo de México, 1996.

Cárdenas Gracia, Jaime F. *Una Constitución para la democracia: Propuestas para un nuevo orden constitucional.* Mexico City: Instituto de Investigaciones Jurídicas, Universidad Nacional Autónoma de México, 1996.

———. *Transición política y reforma constitucional en México.* Mexico City: Universidad Nacional Autónoma de México, 1994.

Careaga, Maite. "El Fracaso de la reforma reeleccionista de 1964." Manuscript, n.d.

———. "Reformas institucionales que fracasan: El Caso de la reforma reeleccionista en el Congreso Mexicano, 1964–1965." B.A. thesis, Instituto Tecnológico Autónomo de México, 1996.

Carey, John M. "Strong Candidates for a Limited Office: Presidentialism and Political Parties in Costa Rica." In *Presidentialism and Democracy in Latin America*, edited by Scott Mainwaring and Matthew Soberg Shugart. Cambridge and New York: Cambridge University Press, 1997.

Carmagnani, Marcello. *Estado y mercado: La Economía pública del liberalismo mexicano, 1850–1911.* Mexico City: Fondo de Cultura Económica, 1994.

Carpizo, Jorge. *El Presidencialismo mexicano.* Mexico City: Siglo XXI Editores, 1978.

Casar, María Amparo. "Las Bases político-institucionales del poder presidencial en México." *Política y Gobierno* 1, no. 1 (1996).

———. "Los Presidentes y secretaríos generales del PRI." *Reforma* (Special Supplement: *Enfoque*), September 28, 1997.

———. "Las Relaciones entre el Poder Ejecutivo y el Legislativo: El Caso de México." *Política y Gobierno* 6, no. 1 (1999).

Castillo Ayala, Javier. "La Contaduría Mayor de Hacienda y el control externo en México." *Auditoría Pública,* 2, no. 3 (March 1992).

Centeno, Miguel Angel. *Democracy Within Reason: Technocratic Revolution in Mexico.* Philadelphia: Pennsylvania State University Press, 1994.

Centro de Investigación para el Desarrollo, A.C. *Reforma del sistema político mexicano.* Mexico City: Editorial Diana, n.d.

Cepeda, Neri Alvaro. "La Contaduría Mayor de Hacienda: Legislación y Análisis. B.A. thesis, Universidad Autónoma de Guadalajara, 1974.

Christlieb Ibarrola, Adolfo. *Crónicas de la no-reelección.* Mexico City: Ediciones de Acción Nacional, 1965.

Contaduría Mayor de Hacienda de México. *La Contaduría Mayor de Hacienda.* Mexico City: Cámara de Diputados, n.d.

Converse, Jean M., and Stanley Presser. *Survey Questions: Handcrafting the Standardized Questionnaire.* Newbury Park, Calif.: Sage Publications, 1986.

Córdova, Arnaldo. *La Formación del poder político en México.* Mexico City: Ediciones Era, 1993 [1972].

Cornelius, Wayne A., and Ann L. Craig. *The Mexican Political System in Transition.* San Diego: Center for U.S.-Mexican Studies, University of California at San Diego, 1991.

Cornelius, Wayne A., Judith Gentleman, and Peter H. Smith, eds. *Mexico's Alternative Political Futures.* San Diego: Center for U.S.-Mexican Studies, University of California at San Diego, 1989.

Cosío Villegas, Daniel. *La Constitución de 1857 y sus críticos.* Mexico City, 1957.

———. *El Sistema político mexicano.* Mexico City: Editorial Joaquín Mortiz, 1972.

———. *La Sucesión presidencial en México.* Mexico City: Editorial Joaquín Mortiz, 1975.

Crepaz, Markus M.L. "Of Principals, Agents, and the Decline of Austrian Corporatism: Anatomy of Legitimacy Crises in a Highly Corporatist System." Paper presented at the 90th Annual Meeting of the American Political Science Association, New York, August 1994.

Crespo, José Antonio. *Jaque al rey: Hacia un nuevo presidencialismo en México.* Mexico City: Editorial Joaquín Mortiz, 1996.

Davis, James A. *The Logic of Causal Order.* Newbury Park, Calif.: Sage Publications, 1985.

De la Garza, Rudolph. "The Mexican Chamber of Deputies and the Mexican Political System." Ph.D. diss., University of Arizona, 1972.

Demsetz, Harold. "The Theory of the Firm Revisited." In *The Nature of the Firm: Origins, Evolution, and Development,* edited by Oliver E. Williamson and Sidney G. Winter. Oxford and New York: Oxford University Press, 1991.

Díaz Cayeros, Alberto, and Beatriz Magaloni. "Autoridad presupuestal del Poder Legislativo en México: Una Primera aproximación." *Política y Gobierno* 5, no. 2 (1998): pp. 503–28.

Diccionario biográfico del gobierno mexicano. Mexico City: Presidencia de la República, 1984, 1987, 1989, 1992.

DiMaggio, Paul J., and Walter W. Powell, eds. Introduction to *The New Institutionalism in Organizational Analysis.* Chicago: University of Chicago Press, 1991.

Edwards, George C., III, John H. Kessel, and Bert A. Rockman, eds. *Researching the Presidency.* Pittsburgh and London: University of Pittsburgh Press, 1993.

Eggertsson, Thráinn. *Economic Behavior and Institutions.* Cambridge and New York: Cambridge University Press, 1990.

Epstein, David, and Sharyn O'Halloran. "Administrative Procedures, Information, and Agency Discretion: Slack Versus Flexibil-
ity." Manuscript, Columbia University, 1993.

———. *Delegating Powers: A Transaction Cost Politics Approach
to Policy Making Under Separate Powers.* Cambridge and New
York: Cambridge University Press, 1999.

———. "The President, Congress, and the Bureaucracy: A Theory
of Transaction Cost Politics." Paper presented at the 91st Annual
Meeting of the American Political Science Association, Chicago,
August 1995.

Fama, E., and M. Jensen. "Separation of Ownership and Control."
Journal of Law and Economics 26 (1983): 301–26.

Ferehohn, John, and Charles Shipan. "Congressional Influence on
Bureaucracy." *Journal of Law, Economics, and Organizations* 6, no. 1
(1990): 1–43.

Fiorina, Morris P. "Congressional Control of the Bureaucracy: A
Mismatch of Incentives and Capabilities." In *Congress Reconsid-
ered*, edited by Lawrence C. Dodd. 2nd ed. Washington, D.C.:
Congressional Quarterly, 1981.

Froman, Lewis A., Jr. *The Congressional Process: Strategies, Rules
and Procedures.* Boston: Little, Brown and Company, n.d.

Gabbert, Jack B. "The Mexican Chief Executive." In *Chief Executives:
National Political Leadership in the United States, Mexico, Great
Britain, Germany and Japan*, edited by Taketsugu Tsurutani and
Jack B. Gabbert. Spokane: Washington State University Press,
1992.

Garrido, Luis Javier. "The Crisis of *Presidencialismo.*" In *Mexico's
Alternative Political Futures*, edited by Wayne A. Cornelius,
Judith Gentleman, and Peter H. Smith. San Diego: Center for
U.S.-Mexican Studies, University of California at San Diego,
1989.

———. *El Partido de la Revolución Institucionalizada: La Formación
del nuevo estado en México, 1928–1945.* Mexico City: Siglo XXI
Editores, 1982.

Gómez, Pablo. *Los Gastos secretos del presidente.* Mexico City: Editorial Grijalbo, 1996.

González Oropeza, Manuel. "Comentario al Articulo 83." In Cámara de Diputados, 55 Legislatura, *Derechos del pueblo mexicano: México a través de sus constituciones*, Vol. 9. Mexico City: Cámara de Diputados, 1994.

Gutiérrez Sergio Elias, and Roberto Rives. *La Constitución Mexicana al final del siglo XX*. 2nd edition. Mexico City: Las Líneas del Mar, S.A. de C.V. 1995.

Guzmán, León. "El Sistema de dos cámaras y sus consecuensias." *Estudios Parlamentarios* 2, no. 1 (August–November 1992). (Originally published in 1870.)

Halpert, Leon. "Legislative Oversight and the Partisan Composition of Government." *Presidential Studies Quarterly* 11, no. 1 (1981): 479–91.

Hamilton, James, and Christopher Schroeder. "Strategic Regulators and the Choice of Rulemaking Procedures: The Selection of Formal versus Informal Rules in Regulating Hazardous Waste." *Law and Contemporary Problems* 57 (1994): 111–60.

Harris, Joseph P. *Congressional Control of the Administration*. Washington, D.C.: The Brookings Institution, 1964.

Havens, Harry S. *The Evolution of the General Accounting Office: From Voucher Audits to Program Evaluations*. Washington, D.C.: U.S. General Accounting Office, 1990.

Hernández Chávez, Alicia. *La Nueva Relación entre Legislativo y Ejecutivo: La Política económica 1982–1997*. Mexico City: Instituto de Investigaciones Legislativas de la Cámara de Diputados, Instituto Politécnico Nacional, Colegio de México and Fondo de Cultura Económica, 1998.

———. "La Parábola del presidencialismo mexicano." In *Presidencialismo y sistema político: México y los Estados Unidos*, edited by Alicia Hernández Chavez. Mexico City: Colegio de México and Fondo de Cultura Económica, 1994.

———, ed. *Presidencialismo y sistema político: México y los Estados Unidos*. Mexico City: Colegio de México and Fondo de Cultura Económica, 1994.

Hernández, Rogelio R. "La División de la élite política mexicana." In *Lecturas 73 del trimestre económico—México: Auge, crisis y ajuste I,* edited by Carlos Bazdrech et al. Mexico City: Fondo de Cultura Económica, 1992.

Hill, Jeffrey, and James Brazier. "Constraining Administrative Decisions." *Journal of Law, Economics, and Organizations* 7 (1991): 373–400.

Horn, Murray, and Kenneth Shepsle. "Commentary on Administrative Arrangements and the Political Control of Agencies: Administrative Process and Organizational Form as Legislative Responses to Agency Costs." *Virginia Law Review* 75 (1989): 499–505.

Instituto Nacional de Administración Pública. *Revista de Administración Pública* (Special Issue: *La Administración del Congreso General*) 92 (1996).

Jenser, M., and W. Meckling. "The Theory of the Firm." *Journal of Financial Economics* 3 (1976): 305–60.

Jepperson, Ronald L. "Institutions, Institutional Effects, and Institutionalism." Manuscript, 1991.

Johnson, Kenneth F. "Mexico's Authoritarian Presidency." In *Presidential Power in Latin American Politics,* edited by Thomas V. DeBacco. New York: Praeger Publishers, 1977.

Kaiser, Fred. "Oversight of Foreign Policy: The U.S. House Committee on International Relations." *Legislative Studies Quarterly* 2 (1977): 255–79.

Keohane, Robert. "Neoliberal Institutionalism: A Perspective on World Politics." In *International Institutions and State Power,* edited by Robert Keohane. Boulder, Colo.: Westview Press, 1989.

———. ed. *International Institutions and State Power.* Boulder, Colo.: Westview Press, 1989.

Kiewiet, Roderick, and Mathew D. McCubbins. "Appropriations Decisions as a Bilateral Bargaining Game Between President and Congress." *Legislative Studies Quarterly* 10 (1985): 181–201.

———. *The Logic of Delegation: Congressional Parties and the Appropriations Process.* Chicago: University of Chicago Press, 1991.

King, Anthony. "Modes of Executive-Legislative Relations: Great Britain, France, and West Germany." *Legislative Studies Quarterly* 1 (1976): 11–36.

Knapp, Frank A. *Parliamentary Government and the Mexican Constitution of 1857: A Forgotten Phase of Mexican Political History.* San Diego: Center for U.S.-Mexican Studies, University of California at San Diego, 1953.

Krauze, Enrique. *La Presidencia imperial: Ascenso y caída del sistema político mexicano, 1940–96.* Mexico City: Tusquets Editores, 1997.

Krehbiel, Keith. 1990. "Are Congressional Committees Composed of Preference Outliers? *American Political Science Review* 84 (1990): 151–163.

—————. *Information and Legislative Organization.* Ann Arbor: University of Michigan Press, 1991.

Lanz Cárdenas, José T. *La Contraloría y el control interno en México.* Mexico City: Fondo de Cultura Económica, 1987.

Lees, John D. "Legislatures and Oversight: A Review Article on a Neglected Area of Research." *Legislative Studies Quarterly* 2 (1977): 193–208.

Linz, Juan J. "The Perils of Presidentialism." *Journal of Democracy* 1 (Winter 1990).

Loaeza, Soledad, and Rafael Segovia, eds. *La Vida mexicana en la crisis.* Mexico City: Colegio de México, 1987.

Lohmann, Susanne, and Sharyn O'Halloran. "Divided Government and U.S. Trade Policy: Theory and Evidence." *International Organization* 48, no. 4 (Autumn 1994): 596–632.

López Portillo y Rojas, José. "El Congreso en el Porfiriato." In *Elevación y caída de Porfirio Díaz.* Mexico City: Editorial Miguel Angel Porrúa, 1975 [1921].

Lujambio, Alonso. "Adios a la excepcionalidad: Régimen presidencial y gobierno dividido en México." *Este País* 10 (February 2000).

—————. "La Cámara de Diputados en México: Arreglos institucionales y proceso político." In *Federalismo y Congreso,* edited by Alonso Lujambio. Mexico City: Universidad Nacional Autónoma de México, 1995.

—————. "Compartir el poder: Gobiernos divididos." *Reforma* (Special Supplement: *Enfoque*), May 25, 1997.

————. "Entre Pasado y futuro: La Ciencia política y el Poder Legislativo en México." *Estudios* 54 (Autumn 1998).

————. "Para qué Servirían las reelecciónes en México?" *Quórum*, April 1993.

————. "La Reelección de los legisladores: Las Ventajas y los dilemas." *Quórum*, January 1996.

————. "Reelección legislativa y estabilidad democrática." *Estudios* (1992).

————, ed. *Federalismo y Congreso*. Mexico City: Universidad Nacional Autónoma de México, 1995.

Lupia, Arthur, and Mathew McCubbins. "Designing Bureaucratic Accountability." *Law and Contemporary Problems* 57 (1994): 91–126.

Madrazo, Carlos. *La Tesis contra la reelección immediata de los diputados y senadores del Congreso de la Unión*. Mexico City: Partido Revolucionario Institucional, 1965.

Mainwaring, Scott, and Matthew Soberg Shugart, eds. *Presidentialism and Democracy in Latin America*. Cambridge and New York: Cambridge University Press, 1997.

Martínez Assad, Carlos, and Alvaro Arreola. "El Poder de los gobernadores." In *La Vida mexicana en la crisis*, edited by Soledad Loaeza and Rafael Segovia. Mexico City: Colegio de México, 1987.

Martínez Gallardo, Cecilia. *Las Legislaturas pequeñas: La Evolución del sistema de comisiones en la Cámara de Diputados, 1824–2000*. B.A. thesis, Instituto Tecnológico Autónomo de México, 1998.

Marván Laborde, Ignacio. *Y Después del presidencialismo? Reflexiones para la formación de un nuevo régimen*. Mexico City: Editorial Océano, 1997.

Mayhew, David R. *Congress: The Electorial Connection*. New Haven, Conn.: Yale University Press, 1974.

————. "The Electoral Connection and the Congress." In *Congress: Structure and Policy*, edited by Mathew D. McCubbins and Terry Sullivan. Cambridge and New York: Cambridge University Press, 1987 [1974].

McCubbins, Mathew. "The Legislative Design of Regulatory Procedure." *American Journal of Political Science* 29 (1985): 721–48.

———. "Positive and Normative Models of Procedural Rights: An Integrative Approach to Administrative Procedures." *Journal of Law, Economics, and Organizations* (Special Issue) 6 (1990): 307–32.

———. "Public Interest and Structure-Induced Policy." *Journal of Law, Economics, and Organizations* 6 (1990): 203–12.

McCubbins, Mathew, Roger G. Noll, and Barry R. Weingast. "Structure and Process, Politics and Policy: Administrative Arrangements and the Political Control of Agencies." *Virginia Law Review* 75 (1989): 431–82.

McCubbins, Mathew, and Thomas Schwartz. "Congressional Oversight Overlooked: Police Patrols Versus Fire Alarms." *American Journal of Political Science* 28 (1984): 167–79.

McCubbins, Mathew, and Terry Sullivan. "Administrative Procedures as Instruments of Political Control." *Journal of Law, Economics, and Organizations* 3 (1987): 243–77.

———, eds. *Congress: Structure and Policy.* Cambridge and New York: Cambridge University Press, 1987.

McManus, John C. "The Costs of Alternative Economic Organizations." *Canadian Journal of Economics* 8 (1975): 334–50.

Mendoza Berrueto, Eliseo. *El Presidencialismo mexicano: Génesis de un sistema imperfecto.* Mexico City: Colegio de la Frontera Norte and Fondo de Cultura Económica, 1996.

Mendoza, Leobardo J. "La Fiscalización de la administración pública en México." M.A. thesis, Facultad Latinoamericana de Ciencias Sociales, 1996.

Meyer, Lorenzo. "El Presidencialismo mexicano: Del Populismo al neoliberalismo." Manuscript, Colegio de México, 1993.

Mezey, Michael L. "Constituency Demands and Legislative Support: An Experiment." *Legislative Studies Quarterly* 1 (1976): 101–28.

———. "Legislatures: Individual Purpose and Institutional Performance." In *Political Science: The State of the Discipline II,* edited by Ada W. Finifter. Washington, D.C.: American Political Science Association, 1993.

Michel Narváez, Jesús. *Reelección legislativa: Tabú*. Mexico City: Editorial Nivi, 1995.

Mijangos Borja, María. "El Control del presupuesto en una democracia." In *El Poder Legislativo en la actualidad*. Mexico City: Cámara de Diputados and Universidad Nacional Autónoma de México, 1994.

———. "La Naturaleza jurídica del presupuesto." *Quórum*, September–October 1987.

Milgrom, Paul, and John Roberts. *Economics, Organization and Management*. Englewood Cliffs, N.J.: Prentice-Hall, 1992.

Mitnick, B. *Political Economy of Regulation*. New York: Columbia University Press, 1980.

Moe, Terry M. "An Assessment of the Positive Theory of 'Congressional Dominance.'" *Legislative Studies Quarterly* 12 (1987): 475–520.

———. "Political Institutions: The Neglected Side of the Story." *Journal of Law, Economics, and Organizations* 6 (1990): 213–53.

———. "The Politics of Bureaucratic Structure." In *Can the Government Govern?* edited by John Chubb and Paul Peterson. Washington, D.C.: The Brookings Institution, 1989.

Molinar Horcasitas, Juan. *El Tiempo de la legitimidad: Elecciones, autoritarismo y democracia en México*. Mexico City: Cal y Arena, 1991.

Mora-Donatto, Cecilia J. *Las Comisiones parlamentarias de investigación como organos de control político*. Mexico City: Cámara de Diputados and Universidad Nacional Autónoma de México, 1998.

Nacif-Hernández, Benito. "The Mexican Chamber of Deputies: The Political Significance of Non-Consecutive Re-election." Ph.D. diss., Faculty of Social Studies, Oxford University, 1995.

———. "La No Reelección legislativa." *Diálogo y Debate de Cultura Política*, July–September 1997.

———. "La Rotación de cargos legislativos y la evolución del sistema de partidos en México." *Política y Gobierno* 4, no. 1 (1997).

Norris, Pipa. *Passages to Power: Legislative Recruitment in Advanced Democracies*. Cambridge and New York: Cambridge University Press, 1997.

North, Douglass C. *Institutions, Institutional Change, and Economic Performance.* Cambridge and New York: Cambridge University Press, 1990.

Ogul, Morris S. *Congress Oversees the Bureaucracy: Studies in Legislative Supervision.* Pittsburgh: University of Pittsburgh Press, 1976.

———. "Congressional Oversight: Structures and Incentives." In *Congress Reconsidered.* 2nd ed., edited by Lawrence C. Dodd. Washington, D.C.: Congressional Quarterly, 1981.

Ogul, Morris S., and Bert A. Rockman. "Overseeing Oversight: New Departures and Old Problems." *Legislative Studies Quarterly* 15 (1990): 5–24.

Orozco Henríquez, Jesús. "Estudio comparativo sobre el órgano legislativo en América Latina." *Revista Mexicana de Estudios Parlamentarios,* January–April 1991.

———. "Las Legislaturas y sus funciones de control sobre la actividad gubernamental." In Senado de la Réplica, *Política y proceso legislativos.* Mexico City: Universidad Nacional Autónoma de México and Editorial Miguel Angel Porrúa, 1985.

———. "El Sistema presidencial en el constituyente de Querétaro y su evolución posterior." In *El Sistema presidencial mexicano.* Mexico City: Instituto de Investigaciones Jurídicas, Universidad Nacional Autónoma de México, 1988.

Osornio Corres, Francisco J. "Estructura funcional y orgánica del Ejecutivo Federal en México." In *El Sistema presidencial mexicano.* Mexico City: Instituto de Investigaciones Jurídicas, Universidad Nacional Autónoma de México, 1988.

Pantoja, David. "Gobierno dividido en México: El Riesgo de la ineficiencia." *Este País* 7 (June 1997).

Pasalagua, Juan Manuel. "Los Organos internos de control." *Auditoría Pública* 2, no. 3 (March 1992).

Patterson, Samuel C. *Congressional Committee Professional Staffing: Capabilities and Constraints.* N.p., n.d.

Pérez, Carlos. *Empresas públicas: Aspectos económicos.* Mexico City: Centro de Investigación y Docencia Económicas, 1976.

Philip, George. *The Presidency in Mexican Politics.* New York: St. Martin's Press, 1992.

Piccato, Pablo. *Congreso y revolución: Ensayo.* Mexico City: Instituto Nacional de Estudios Históricos de la Revolución Mexicana, Secretaría de Gobernación, 1991.

Pichardo Pagaza, Ignacio. "Función de control y evaluación." In *Introducción a la administración pública de México,* Vol. 2: *Funciones y especialidades.* Mexico City: Instituto Nacional de Administración Pública, 1984.

————. *Ley Orgánica de la Administración Pública Federal.* Mexico City, n.d.

————. *Reflexiones sobre el proceso presupuestal en la Cámara de Diputados: Un Enfoque comparativo.* Mexico City: Instituto Nacional de Administración Pública, 1981.

Polsby, Nelson W. "Legislatures." In *Handbook of Political Science,* edited by F. Greenstein and N. Polsby. Reading, Mass.: Addison-Wesley, 1975.

Rabasa, Emilio O. *La Constitución y la dictadura.* Mexico City, 1912.

————, comp. *Nuestra Constitución: Del Poder Ejecutivo; De la División de poderes y del Poder Legislativo; De la Iniciativa y formación de las leyes; De las Facultades del Congreso y de la comisión permanente.* Mexico City: Instituto Nacional de Estudios Históricos de la Revolución Mexicana, Secretaría de Gobernación, 1991.

Raigosa Sotelo, Luis. "Las Comisiones parlamentarias en el Congreso mexicano." *Revista Mexicana de Estudios Parlamentarios,* January–April 1991.

Ramírez, Gilberto, and E. Salim. *La Clase política mexicana.* Mexico City: EDAMEX, 1987.

Reyes Heroles, Federico. "Porqué del presidencialismo." *Diálogo y Debate de Cultura Política,* July–September 1997.

Robinson, Glen. "Commentary on Administrative Arrangements and the Political Control of Agencies: Political Uses of Structure and Process." *Virginia Law Review* 75 (1989): 483–98.

Rockman, Bert A. "Legislative-Executive Relations and Legislative Oversight." *Legislative Studies Quarterly* 9 (1984): 387–440.

Rodríguez Lozano, Amador. "La Reforma del Estado y el Congreso de la Unión: Una Visión desde el Senado sobre el fortalecimiento del Poder Legislativo en México." *Revista del Senado de la República* 1, no. 3 (April–June 1996).

Rogozinski, Jacques, and Francisco J. Casas. "The Restructuring Process in Mexico." In *Public Administration in Mexico Today,* compiled by María E. Vázquez Nava. Mexico City: Secretaría de la Contraloría de la Federación and Fondo de Cultura Económica, 1993.

Rosen, Bernard. *Holding Government Bureaucracies Accountable.* 2nd ed. New York: Praeger Publishers, 1989.

Rosenthal, Alan. "Legislative Behavior and Legislative Oversight." *Legislative Studies Quarterly* 6 (1981): 115–31.

Rubio, Francisco. "El Control parlamentario." *Revista Mexicana de Estudios Parlamentarios,* January–April 1991.

Ruiz Massieu, José F. "Las Relaciones entre el Poder Ejecutivo y el Congreso de la Unión: El Trabajo legislativo, el control político y la planeación legislativa." In Senado de la República, *Política y proceso legislativos.* Mexico City: Universidad Nacional Autónoma de México and Editorial Miguel Angel Porrúa, 1985.

Salazar Abaroa, Enrique A. *Derecho parlamentario: La Contaduría Mayor de Hacienda hacia un Tribunal Mayor de Hacienda.* Mexico City: Instituto Nacional de Administración Pública, 1989.

Sánchez Susarrey, Jaime. *La Transición incierta.* Mexico City: Editorial Vuelta, 1991.

Sartori, Giovanni. *Comparative Constitutional Engineering: An Inquiry into Structures, Incentives, and Outcomes.* New York: New York University Press, 1994.

Scher, Seymour. "Conditions for Legislative Control." *Journal of Politics* 25 (1963): 526–51.

Scherer, Julio. *Los Presidentes.* Mexico City: Editorial Grijalbo, 1995.

Shepsle, Kenneth A. "The Changing Textbook Congress." In *Can the Government Govern?* edited by John E Chubb and Paul E. Peterson. Washington, D.C.: The Brookings Institution, 1989.

Shepsle, Kenneth A., and Barry R. Weingast. *Positive Theories of Congressional Institutions.* Ann Arbor: University of Michigan Press, 1995.

Shugart, Matthew Soberg, and John M. Carey. *Presidents and Assemblies: Constitutional Design and Electoral Dynamics*. Cambridge and New York: Cambridge University Press, 1992.

Shughart, William F., II, Robert D. Tollison, and Brian L.Goff. "Bureaucratic Structure and Congressional Control." *Southern Economic Journal* 52 (1986): 199–210.

Smith, Peter. "The 1988 Presidential Succession in Historical Perspective." In *Mexico's Alternative Political Futures*, edited by Wayne A. Cornelius, Judith Gentleman, and Peter H. Smith. San Diego: Center for U.S.-Mexican Studies, University of California at San Diego, 1989.

Smith, Steven S., and Christopher J. Deering. *Committees in Congress*. 2nd ed. Washington, D.C.: Congressional Quarterly, 1990.

Sordo, Reynaldo. *El Congreso en la Primera República Centralista*. Mexico City: Colegio de México and Instituto Tecnológico Autónomo de México, 1993.

Spiller, Pablo T. "Politicians, Interest Groups, and Regulators: A Multiple-Principals Agency Theory of Regulators or 'Let Them Be Bribed.'" *Journal of Law and Economics* 33 (1990): 65–101.

Stiglitz, Joseph E. "Principal and Agent." In *The New Palgrave*, edited by John Eatwell. New York: Norton, 1989.

Suárez Farías, Francisco. *Elite, tecnocracia y movilidad política en México*. Mexico City: Universidad Autónoma Metropolitana, Xochimilco, 1991.

Tena Ramírez, Felipe. *Derecho constitucional mexicano*. Mexico City: Editorial Miguel Angel Porrúa, 1994.

Torres, Zubia. *La Politíca y el Poder Legislativo*. Mexico City, 1963.

Ugalde, Luis Carlos. "Los Aspectos legislativos del gasto público en México, 1970–96." *Perfiles Latinoamericanos,* 6 (June 10, 1997).

———. "Consideraciones sobre la reelección en México." *Nexos*, 15 (May 1992).

———. "El Poder fiscalizador de la Cámara de Diputados en México." In *El control de las finanzas públicas*, edited by Gilberto Rincón Gallardo. Mexico City: Centro de Estudios para la Reforma del Estado, 1996.

————. "Requieren asesores y reelección: Diputados de la 57 Legislatura." *Reforma*, December 16, 1997.

————. "Vigilando a los gobernantes." *Reforma* (Special Supplement: *Enfoque*), July 4, 1996.

Valadés, Diego. "El Control interorgánico entre los Poderes Legislativo y Ejecutivo de México." In *El Sistema presidencial mexicano*. Mexico City: Instituto de Investigaciones Jurídicas, Universidad Nacional Autónoma de México, 1988.

————. "Las Relaciones de control entre el Legislativo y en Ejecutivo en México." *Revista Mexicana de Estudios Parlamentarios*, January–April 1991.

Vargas, Avalos, Pedro. "El Presupuesto federal: Columna del federalismo y el municipio libre." *Quórum*, September–October 1997.

Vázquez Alfaro, José L. *El Control de la administración pública en México*. Mexico City: Instituto de Investigaciones Jurídicas, Universidad Nacional Autónoma de México, 1996.

Vázquez Nava, María E. "Funciones de la Secretaría de la Contraloría General de la Federación." *Auditoría Pública* 2, no. 3 (1992).

————, comp. *Public Administration in Mexico Today*. Mexico City: Secretaría de la Contraloría de la Federación and Fondo de Cultura Económica, 1993.

Villa Aguilera, Manuel. *La Institución presidencial*. Mexico City: Universidad Nacional Autónoma de México and Editorial Miguel Angel Porrúa, 1987.

Weingast, Barry R. "The Congressional-Bureaucratic System: A Principal-Agent Perspective (with Applications to the SEC)." *Public Choice* 44 (1984): 147–91.

————. "A Rational Choice Perspective on Congressional Norms." *American Journal of Political Science* 23 (1979): 245–62.

Weingast, Barry R., and William J. Marshall. "The Industrial Organization of Congress, or Why Legislatures, Like Firms, Are Not Organized as Markets." *Journal of Political Economy* 96 (1988): 132–63.

Weingast, Barry R., and Mark Moran. "Bureaucratic Discretion or Congressional Control?: Regulatory Policy by the Federal Trade Commission." *Journal of Political Economy* 91 (1983): 765–800.

Weldon, Jeffrey. "The Legal and Partisan Framework of the Legislative Delegation of the Budget in Mexico." Manuscript, Instituto Tecnológico Autónomo de México, 1999.

———. "Political Sources of *Presidencialismo* in Mexico." In *Presidentialism and Democracy in Latin America*, edited by Scott Mainwaring and Matthew Soberg Shugart. Cambridge and New York: Cambridge University Press, 1997.

———. "El Proceso presupuestario en México: Defendiendo el poder del bolsillo." *Perfiles Latinoamericanos* 6 (June 10, 1997).

———. Untitled manuscript, 1994.

West, William F. *Controlling the Bureaucracy: Institutional Constraints in Theory and Practice.* New York: M. E. Sharpe, 1995.

Wood, Dan B. "Principals, Bureaucrats, and Responsiveness in Clean Air Enforcement." *American Political Science Review* 82 (1988): 213–34.

Wood, Dan B., and Richard W. Waterman. "The Dynamics of Political Control of the Bureaucracy." *American Political Science Review* 85 (1991): 801–28.

Zaid, Gabriel. *La Economía presidencial.* Mexico City: Editorial Vuelta, 1987.

Zamora, Guillermo. *Caso CONASUPO: La Leche radiactiva.* Mexico City: Planeta, 1997.

Zegbe Sanen, Alfonso. *Política y proceso legislativos.* Mexico City: Editorial Miguel Angel Porrúa, 1985.

Zorrilla Martínez, Pedro G. "Las Relaciones entre los Poderes Ejecutivo y Legislativo." *Quórum*, September–October 1994.

LAWS

Cámara de Diputados. *Derechos del pueblo mexicano: México a través de sus constituciones*, Vols. 7, 8, and 9. Mexico City: Cámara de Diputados, 55 Legislatura, 1994.

Constitución Política de los Estados Unidos Mexicanos. Mexico City: Editorial Miguel Angel Porrúa, 1999.

Ley de Adquisiciones y Obras Públicas (Law of Government Purchases and Public Works). In *Legislación de la Administración Pública Federal*. Mexico City: Ediciones Delma, 1995.

Ley Federal de Entidades Paraestateles (Federal Law of Semi-State Entities). In *Legislación de la Administración Pública Federal*. Mexico City: Ediciones Delma, 1995.

Ley Federal de Responsabilidades de los Servidores Públicos (Federal Law of Civil Servants' Responsibilities). In *Legislación de la Administración Pública Federal*. Mexico City: Ediciones Delma, 1995.

Ley General de Deuda Pública (General Law of Public Debt). In *Legislación de la Administración Pública Federal*. Mexico City: Ediciones Delma, 1995.

Ley Orgánica de la Administración Pública Federal (Federal Law of the Federal Public Administration). In *Legislación de la Administración Pública Federal*. Mexico City: Ediciones Delma, 1995.

Ley Orgánica del Congreso de los Estados Unidos Mexicanos (Federal Law of the Mexican Congress). Mexico City: Congreso de la Unión, n.d.

Ley Orgánica de la Contaduría Mayor de Hacienda (Federal Law of the Treasury Accounting Office). Mexico City: Contaduría Mayor de Hacienda, n.d.

Ley de Presupuesto, Contabilidad y Gasto Público (Law of Budget, Accounting, and Public Spending). In *Legislación de la Administración Pública Federal*. Mexico City: Ediciones Delma, 1995.

Proyecto de Nueva Ley de Presupuesto, Contabilidad y Gasto Público (Law of Budget, Accounting, and Public Spending, as approved by the Chamber of Deputies on April 1999).

Rabasa, Emilio O., comp. *Nuestra Constitución: Del Poder Ejecutivo; De la División de Poderes y del Poder Legislativo; De la Iniciativa y Formación de las Leyes; De las Facultades del Congreso y de la Comisión Permanente*. Mexico City: Instituto Nacional de

Estudios Históricos de la Revolución Mexicana, Secretaría de Gobernación, 1991.

Reglamento Interior de la Contaduría Mayor de Hacienda (Bylaw). Mexico City: Contaduría Mayor de Hacienda, n.d.

Reglamento Interior del Congreso de los Estados Unidos Mexicanos (Bylaw). Mexico City: Congreso de la Unión, n.d.

DOCUMENTS

Cámara de Diputados. *Composición de la LVI Legislatura de la Cámara de Diputados (Cuadernos de Apoyo)*. Mexico City: Comite de Biblioteca, Cámara de Diputados, 1995.

———. *Diario de debates* (Diary of Debates). Mexico City, 1969–98.

———. *La Voluntad de Nuestro Pueblo: Memoria de la LV Legislatura*. Mexico City: Cámara de Diputados, 55 Legislatura, 1994.

Congreso de la Unión. *Memoria del Primer Periodo Ordinario de Sesiones, Septiembre-Diciembre 1985*. Mexico City: Congreso de la Union, 53 Legislatura, 1985.

Contaduría Mayor de Hacienda. *Informe Previo de la Cuenta de la Hacienda Pública Federal* (Preliminary Report). Mexico City: Contaduría Mayor de Hacienda, Cámara de Diputados, 1969–93.

———. *Informe de Resultados sobre la Revisión de la Cuenta de la Hacienda Pública Federal*. Mexico City: Contaduría Mayor de Hacienda, Cámara de Diputados, 1969–93.

Diario oficial de la Federación. Mexico City, various years.

Instituto Nacional de Estadística, Geografía e Informática (INEGI). *Estadísticas Históricas de México*, Vol. 2. Mexico City: INEGI, 1994.

Legislación de la Administración Pública Federal, 1995. Mexico City: Ediciones Delma, 1995.

Presidencia de la República. *Manual de Organización de la Administración Pública Federal*. Mexico City: Presidencia de la República, 1982.

Secretaría de Hacienda. *Cuenta de la Hacienda Pública Federal*

(Public Account). Mexico City, various years.

———. *Presupuesto de Egresos* (Budget Bill). Mexico City, various years.

———. *El Proceso de Enajenación de Entidades Paraestatales.* Mexico City: Secretaría de Hacienda y Crédito Público, 1994.

Senado de la República. *Iniciativa para el fortalecimiento del Poder Legislativo* (Proceedings of the Senate of the Republic). Mexico City, various years.

———. *Politica y proceso legislativos.* Mexico City: Universidad Nacional Autónoma de México and Editorial Miguel Angel Porrúa, various years.

NEWSPAPERS AND MAGAZINES

El Día
Excélsior
El Financiero
La Jornada
Proceso
Reforma
El Universal
Uno Más Uno

ACRONYMS AND ABBREVIATIONS

ASF — *Auditoría Superior de la Federación* (Federal Auditing Office)

BANPESCA — *Banco Nacional de Pesca* (National Bank of Fishing)

CD — *Centro Democrático* (Democratic Center)

CFE — *Comisión Federal de Electricidad* (Federal Electricity Commission)

CIDE — *Centro de Investigación y Docencia Económicas* (Center for Research and Economic Policy)

CMH — *Contaduría Mayor de Hacienda* (Treasury Accounting Office)

CONASUPO— *Comisión Nacional de Subsidios Populares* (National Commission for Popular Assistance)

FDN — *Frente Democrático Nacional* (National Democratic Front)

IFE — *Instituto Federal Electoral* (Federal Electoral Institute)

IMSS — *Instituto Mexicano del Seguro Social* (Mexican Institute for Social Security)

INFONAVIT — *Instituto Nacional de Fomento para la Vivienda de los Trabajadores* (National Employees' Housing Fund)

LFC — *Luz y Fuerza del Centro* (Electricity and Energy of the Center)

PAN — *Partido Acción Nacional* (National Action Party)

PARM — *Partido Auténtico de la Revolución Mexicana* (Authentic Mexican Revolutionary Party)

PAS — *Partido de Acción Social* (Social Action Party)
PCM — *Partido Comunista Mexicano* (Mexican Communist Party)
PDM — *Partido Demócrata Mexicano* (Mexican Democracy Party)
PEF — *Presupuesto de Egresos de la Federación* (Federal Budget)
PEMEX — *Petróleos Mexicanos* (Mexican Petroleum Company)
PMS — *Partido Mexicano Socialista* (Mexican Socialist Party)
PNR — *Partido Nacional Revolucionario* (National Revolutionary Party)
POA — *Programa Operativo Anual* (Annual Operations Program)
PPS — *Partido Popular Socialista* (Socialist Popular Party)
PRD — *Partido de la Revolución Democrática* (Democratic Revolutionary Party)
PRI — *Partido Revolucionario Institucional* (Institutional Revolutionary Party)
PRM — *Partido de la Revolución Mexicana* (Mexican Revolution Party)
PSN — *Partido de la Sociedad Nacionalista* (National Society Party)
PST — *Partido Socialista de los Trabajadores* (Socialist Labor Party)
PSUM — *Partido Social Unificado de México* (United Socialist Party of Mexico)
PT — *Partido del Trabajo* (Labor Party)
PVEM — *Partido Verde Ecologista de México* (Green Party of Mexico)
SEDESOL — *Secretaría de Desarrollo Social* (Secretariat of Social Development)
TELMEX — *Teléfonos de México* (Telephone Company of Mexico)
UNAM — *Universidad Nacional Autónoma de México* (National Autonomous University of Mexico)

INDEX

Page numbers followed by the letters f, t and n refer to figures, tables, and notes.

executive branch (*continued*)
    factors contributing to lack of
        accountability in, 163–64
    preparation for submission of
        budget bill, 22
    role of new Congress in
        overseeing and controlling,
        162–63
    See also president

Federal Auditing Office. *See* ASF
    (Federal Auditing Office)
Federal Electricity Commission.
    See CFE (Federal Electricity
    Commission)
Fox, Vicente
    election of (2000), 2, 144
    as leader of PAN, 2
    on legislation to permit
        consecutive reelection, 6,
        115–16
    as legislator, 107
    political resources as president,
        121–22, 137
    post-election economic
        proposals, 24
    power on assumption of
        presidency, 127, 135–36
    on restoration of consecutive
        reelection, 115

Gabbert, Jack B., 122
Galicia Estrada, Pedro, 74
García Sainz, Ricardo, 41
García Villa, Juan A., 47, 52, 147
Gómez, Pablo, 68
González, Rodolfo, 39
Guerrero, Gregorio, 39
Gurría, Angel, 90–91

Hernández Chavez, Alicia, 134–35
Herrán, José, 89
Hinojosa, Manuel, 83

INFONAVIT investigation, 78–79
Institutional Revolutionary Party.
    See PRI (Institutional Revolu-
    tionary Party)

Knapp, Frank A., 4

Labastida, Francisco, 107, 115,
    137, 167
Laguna Verde nuclear power
    plant, 69–70
Lanz, Trinidad, 72
legal system
    interpretation of presidential
        veto power, 32
    legal changes to presidential
        appointment powers, 136
    omissions related to budget bill
        approval, 31–32
    Senate exclusion from budget
        process, 33–34
    studies related to congressional
        powers, 4–5
legislation
    creating ASF, 51, 54
    required agency progress
        reports, 44
legislative oversight
    of budget by Chamber of
        Deputies, 20–21
    causes of infrequent and
        ineffective, 164–67
    congressional investigative
        committees, 62–66

state-owned enterprises
(*continued*)
Supervisory Committee. *See*
Chamber of Deputies

TELMEX, 67–69, 87–88
Tena, Felipe, 4, 33–34
Treasury Accounting Office. *See*
CMH (Treasury Accounting
Office)

Vásquez Nava, María Elena, 85
Velasco, Cuauhtémoc, 89

Weldon, Jeffrey, 26, 32, 99–100

Yañez, Ismael, 69

Zedillo, Ernesto, 39, 81, 83
contributions to democracy in
Mexico, 136–37
diminished partisan powers of,
167
post-1997 political opposition
to, 144
reforms to informal partisan
powers during regime of,
136–38

ABOUT THE AUTHOR

LUIS CARLOS UGALDE is chief of staff to Mexico's ambassador to the United States of America. He previously served in the same capacity for the minister of energy in Mexico, for whom he also worked as an adviser on political and economic affairs. Ugalde has held positions in several other agencies in the Mexican government, including the National Bank for Public Services and Public Works (BANOBRAS) and the Technical Secretariat of the Economic Cabinet in the Office of the President. In addition, Ugalde has been adjunct professor of international affairs at American University in Washington, D.C., and professor of economics, political science, and international management at the Autonomous Technological Institute of Mexico (ITAM), the Center for Economic Research and Training (CIDE), and the Matías Romero Institute for Diplomatic Studies in Mexico City. Ugalde received his Ph.D. in political science from Columbia University, master's degrees in public administration and political science from the same institution, and a B.A. in economics from ITAM. His publications include *Vigilando al Ejecutivo* (published jointly by the Mexican Chamber of Deputies and Miguel Angel Porrúa in 2000) as well as articles in books, journals, and periodicals published in Mexico, including *Reforma* daily, *Nexos*, and *Este País*. He has also been a regular contributor to *El Financiero* daily and *Uno Más Uno* daily.